Critique of Lean

Pathway to Improvement

The Critic, 1916
Lajos Tihanyi (1885-1938)
Brooklyn Museum

Bob Emiliani

Critique of Lean: Pathway to Improvement / Bob Emiliani

ISBN-13: 978-0-9898631-7-9

Library of Congress Control Number: 2017903498

1. Business 2. Management 3. Economics 4. Toyota 5. Lean

First Edition: March 2017

Published by The CLBM, LLC, South Kingstown, Rhode Island, USA

Information contained in this book originated from the bobemiliani.com blog and has been edited, revised, corrected, expanded, and condensed to improve clarity, accuracy, and readability.

This publication provides accurate information with respect to the subject matter covered. It is sold with the understanding that it does not in any way represent legal, financial, business, consulting, or other professional service.

Manufactured using digital print-on-demand technology.

"Find a subject to think about, stare at an object until a hole is almost bored through it, and find out its essential nature."

- Taiichi Ohno

Toyota Production System House

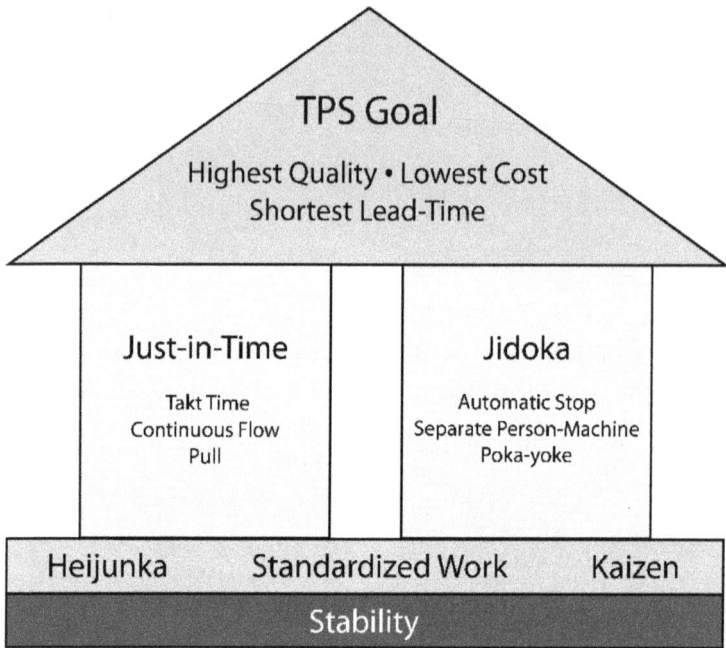

TPS Goal

Highest Quality • Lowest Cost
Shortest Lead-Time

Just-in-Time	Jidoka
Takt Time	Automatic Stop
Continuous Flow	Separate Person-Machine
Pull	Poka-yoke

Heijunka   Standardized Work   Kaizen

Stability

"IE [industrial engineering] is a system and the Toyota production system may be regarded as Toyota-style IE… Unless IE results in cost reductions and profit increases, I think it is meaningless."

- Taiichi Ohno

CONTENTS

"Just remember the tortoise and the hare."

- Taiichi Ohno

Preface

From its humble beginnings in 1988 [1, 2], Lean has become a global phenomenon [3, 4], more widespread and enduring than most people would have ever imagined. Starting as an interpretation of Toyota's production system, and, some 20 years later, as an interpretation of Toyota's overall management system, Lean, in one form or another, has touched thousands of organizations and great numbers of people.

Organizations devoted to the advancement of Lean publish story after story of technical and human success in the practice of Lean. The abundance of Lean success stories easily gives the impression that Lean, while challenging, routinely yields favorable results. So much so, there is not even a need to offer even the simplest cautionary statement such as: "Individual results may vary. Results are not claimed to be typical."

As an interpretation of Toyota's management methods, are the results one can achieve with Lean the same, greater than, or less than what one can achieve through the close practice of Toyota's actual management methods? Are the results from Lean as good as they seem, or have people succumbed to illusions or marketing hype? What is the truth? And what methods can be used to discover the truth?

The purpose of this volume is to critique [5] Lean management using Toyota's management system as the standard comparison. This Ohnoist perspective [6, 7] is a valid basis for comparison because Lean has long been presented to the public by its originators (or, producers), James P. Womack and Daniel T. Jones, as synonymous with Toyota management [1, 2, 4].

Critique of Lean explores important differences between Lean management and Toyota management, which, in turn, reveal opportunities for improving Lean itself and how users understand and practice Lean.

The goal of this volume is to stimulate needed discussion directed towards examining the many gaps between Lean and TPS, and inspire people to improve their understanding and practice of Lean.

Why Critique Lean?

Why does something seemingly so successful as Lean need to be critiqued? Doesn't success speak for itself? Perhaps to some it does. Yet, the most expensive sports cars, award-winning movies, video games, hair dryers, and tooth brushes are critiqued. Everything is critiqued, so why not Lean – both as a product and how it is used? Lean is not a sacred cow, and therefore is not immune to criticism or the need to improve.

But, more importantly, if someone creates and leads a new movement, and people take action based on what movement leaders say, then movement leaders have a great responsibility to get it right, if not from the start, then as soon thereafter as is possible. Errors in movement leaders' understanding and delayed correction can result in tangible harm to people. It also exposes weaknesses that are then subject to harsh criticism from varied sources.

While the purpose of any critique is to thoughtfully identify strengths and weaknesses, the focus is often on weaknesses because they pinpoint clear opportunities for improvement.

Who Benefits?

The principal beneficiaries of critiques are the people who produce Lean (originators and successors) and those consume (use) Lean. By becoming aware of Lean's weaknesses, people can make improvements in order to create a better product and use it to greater positive effect. The hope is that improvements lead to a steady increase in favorable outcomes and a decline in unfavorable outcomes – particularly the most common ones.

Awareness of Lean's strengths and weaknesses is a process that occurs over time, and so the opportunities for improvement reveal themselves over time. The result is continuous improvement in the product, Lean, and its understanding and practice among users. But, that assumes that the people who produce [8, 9] and who consume the Lean are attentive and responsive to criticism. In this volume, I will show that both producer and users have been largely inattentive and unresponsive, and so the results achieved given the effort expended has been much lower that it ought to be.

Who Cares?
Why should anyone care about a critique of Lean whose purpose is to improve the product and its understanding and practice? Both producer and user should care because they seek favorable results. Perhaps more importantly, they claim enduring commitment to facts, seeing with one's own eyes, respect for people [10], and continuous improvement. To achieve that, they must do more than simply embrace success stories. They must also embrace critiques and other types of information that, while uncomfortable, is necessary for them to comprehend and react to.

However, it is not unusual for people to say they are committed to something and then do things that are the opposite, in small or large ways. Hypocrisy is a common feature of the human condition for which there is no sure antidote. But, the harm it can do is clear. Namely, job loss; slowing down or stopping progress; asking people to apply their mental and physical labors under misleading or incomplete circumstances; loss of personal commitment to the practice of Lean; and loss of desire to advance improved methods of management.

Who is Qualified to Critique Lean?

In order to critique something, one must possess sufficient knowledge of the subject matter. Interested readers can view the author's qualifications for critiquing Lean in the Appendix.

• • • • •

A critique is healthy for Lean because it makes people think and improve their practice of Lean, and it is consistent with "Continuous Improvement and "Respect for People." In Lean, critical thinking is called asking "Why?," and we are taught to always ask "Why?" to challenge conventions and preconceptions. That's what we do, isn't it?

And so we must also challenge the conventions and preconceptions of Lean. Though perhaps uncomfortable to some, critiques are a method for moving a field of knowledge forward by helping people to recognize problems, think, prompt them to do research, explore new ideas, and experiment.

People trained in Lean should welcome criticism as they are supposed to be curious about problems, exceptional critical thinkers, skilled problem-solvers, comfortable speaking truth to power, and committed to both "Continuous Improvement and "Respect for People."

While critiques and criticisms can have the appearance of ad hominem attacks, they are not that at all. The work of scholars, leaders in a given field, designers, etc., is subject to close scrutiny, and criticism of their work will necessarily be associated with their name.

Arguing the merits of someone's work requires the identification of those who did the work. But that association does not constitute an ad hominem attack. To be sure, the people who brought us Lean are good people with good intentions, though, as we now know, overconfident in their research and analysis skills.

After decades of receiving critiques of my work in industry and academia by students, peers, superiors, subordinates, customers, suppliers, and many others, I know well that criticism can sting, and I grumble about it as anyone else does. But I have always remained committed to the idea that criticism, whether it is harsh or mild, on-target or off-target, reveals important things about my work that need to be improved.

In addition, I have long been strongly self-critical of my own work. I have found self-criticism to be an extremely effective way to motivate me to rapidly improve my work. It has proven to be a great idea-generator for experimenting and trying new things.

So, let it never be said that I can only deliver criticism but never take criticism. Even if that were true, it is beside the point. My critique of Lean should not suggest to readers a dislike for Lean, its originators, or its users.

My criticism of Lean is rooted in the idea that there is much that can be improved, and that it must be improved faster. Its users must develop a deeper understanding of Lean and practice it with greater skill in order to achieve better results more quickly.

The strengths of Lean are many, but I want to focus on a few that stand out because they impacted so many people:

• Lean helped get people interested in Toyota's management system and made elements of the Toyota production system (TPS) accessible.

- Lean helped people take a greater interest in work, processes, management, and leadership.
- Lean got people interested in process improvement, thereby making their work more interesting and less of a drudgery.
- Lean got people interested in learning and trying new things.
- Lean catalyzed billions of improvements in work processes. The many success stories are not lies – but they are not the whole story either.

However, Lean might have no future if its producer and users are unwilling to recognize and correct its weaknesses, such as outcomes that have not been mutually beneficial between management (capital) and labor. Facing up to the weaknesses and making improvements demonstrates a resect for all people, including those who love Lean and wish to see it survive and prosper.

According to the Lean Enterprise Institute, the "ultimate goal" for Lean "is to provide perfect value to the customer through a perfect value creation process that has zero waste" [7]. In addition to being badly mistaken (i.e. completely unrelated to TPS or Toyota management practice), the goal sets the bar too low. And, with that as its "ultimate goal," Lean continues, as it long has, to be unresponsive to workers' interests.

Lean should strive for a higher goal, such as evolving into a management system that also results in improved human health; that all employees someday leave work physically and mentally healthier than when they arrived. And it should also deliver improved economic outcomes for workers.

This vision might be realized if the producers of Lean and users of Lean are receptive to the critiques contained in this book [11].

Finally, I welcome your thoughts and criticisms.

Bob Emiliani
South Kingstown, Rhode Island
March 2017

• • • • •

Disclosure: Professor Emiliani is not affiliated with, nor does he have any financial interest or contract with, any organization that promotes TPS or Lean management.

• • • • •

Note: Originally, the word "lean" was spelled with a lowercase l. This volume considers Lean a proper noun and uses uppercase L. You will see it both ways in this book depending upon the context: The author's use of the word (uppercase) and its original use or its use by others in passages of text that have been quoted (lowercase).

Introduction

What is the basis for critiquing Lean? As was noted in the Preface, Lean has long been presented to the public as synonymous with Toyota management. "Lean" is said by its producers [1, 2] to be the generic version of Toyota management. Therefore, both are the same. But, are they really the same? Are they exactly the same? Are they similar enough to be considered the same? Are they different, but merely called the same?

A generic product, such as food, paper towels, or over-the-counter medications, are never exactly the same. There is always something missing; something that changes the flavor or effectiveness of the product. Is Lean any different than these common examples? No.

Lean is an English-language interpretation of a system of management unique to Toyota – whose creation was informed by Japanese language, Japanese history, Japanese traditions, Japanese daily living, Shinto and Buddhism, and business conditions in 1950s Japan – yet Lean is said to be the same as Toyota management. How can that be?

Language alone suggests that equivalency between Lean and Toyota management is impossible in part because Japanese and English are so different. This is but one of many things that differentiate the generic brand, Lean management, from the name-brand, Toyota management. Many other important differences exist, suggesting that equivalency between Lean and Toyota management is simply an illusion.

Is it plausible that American- and British-born university researchers would be able to fully – or even partially – comprehend Japanese language, Japanese history, Japanese traditions, Japanese daily living, Shinto and Buddhism, and 1950s business conditions in Japan? Especially, given that the interpretation, Lean, is based on limited, not thorough and continuous study. Evidence of discontinuities in the study of Toyota's management methods appears in later chapters.

Therefore, it's not credible to claim that Lean is synonymous with, or the generic version of, Toyota management. It is, in fact, an unbelievable stretch. Yet, people believe it, and to the detriment of their comprehension and improvement efforts.

Japanese veterans of Toyota struggle to explain TPS, so how can American and British university researchers explain it? Fujio Cho, one of Taiichi Ohno's team members and a former Toyota president and chairman, said [3]:

> "Our way of thinking is very difficult
> to copy or even to understand."

Indeed it is. Katsuaki Watanabe, another former Toyota president said [4]:

> "There's no end to the process of learning about the
> Toyota Way. I don't think I have a complete
> understanding even today, and I have worked
> for the company for 43 years."

English-speakers raised in "Western" history and traditions cannot possibly fathom the nearly countless coarse and fine details that make up Toyota's management practice – nor the idea that nobody can ever know TPS, though anyone can know Lean (see page 161).

Because Lean is based on limited, not thorough, study of Toyota management, the very best one can do is present an approximation based on one's understanding at any point in time.

So, we must dispel popular notions of equivalency. These include:

Toyota Production System ≠ Lean Production
Toyota Management System ≠ Lean Management
Toyota Way ≠ Lean Way
Toyota Thinking ≠ Lean Thinking
Kaizen Thinking ≠ Lean Thinking
Toyota Leadership ≠ Lean Leadership
Etc.

If you accept these inequalities, then you will immediately realize that Lean is a deeply flawed interpretation. This results in six important questions. Namely:

1. How flawed is Lean?
2. How serious are the flaws?
3. Can the flaws be corrected?
4. Will corrections be effective?
5. Can good things be achieved despite the flaws?
6. Is Lean beyond repair?

Before answering these questions, look at the image on the following page, which compares key characteristics of the Toyota Production System to Lean Production. The word "production" is used in keeping with the original formulation and the early interpretations, but you can substitute the word "management" for "production" to no ill effect. The comparison begins in 1988 when the term "Lean" was first introduced [2] and post-1996 after the book *Lean Thinking* [5] was published.

Let me give you an indication of how bad the interpretation is, especially for the "Lean (1996 →)" column: When I show this chart to Japanese colleagues who have extensive practice with TPS and kaizen, they burst out laughing and shake their head. To Ohnoists, Lean is an absurd interpretation of TPS. It is far

Comparison of Toyota Production System and Lean

Method	Toyota Production System	Lean (1988)	Lean (1996→)
Designer	Industrial Engineers	Mechanical Engineer*	Social Scientists**
Goal	Cost Reduction Productivity Improvement	Quality Productivity	Maximize Customer Value
Principles	Continuous Improvement Respect for People	Continuous Improvement	Specify Value Identify the Value Stream Flow Pull Perfection
Normal Condition	Flow	Flow	Perfect Processes
Focus of Improvement	Human	Technical	Technical
Primary Teaching Method	Genba Kaizen	Team Leader	Classroom
Object of Interest	Waste, Unevenness, Unreasonableness	Inventories	Value Creating Activities
Desired Outcome	Customer Satisfaction Survival	High Plant Performance	Perfect Value

* John Krafcik, "Triumph of the Lean Production System" (1988) https://www.lean.org/downloads/MITSloan.pdf
** James P. Womack and Daniel T. Jones, *Lean Thinking* (1996) and http://www.lean.org/WhatsLean/ (accessed 15 March 2017)

off the mark. This reflects a great overconfidence in the understanding of TPS by the producers of Lean.

You should spend a good amount of time contemplating the differences, in detail, between the "Toyota Production System" column and the "Lean (1996 →)" column in terms of:

- How people will think
- What their focus will be
- What they will actually do
- The time-scale
- Business impact (financial and non-financial results)

The comparison of TPS and Lean suggests many important questions:

- Why are there differences between Lean and TPS?
- Why did Lean drift farther away from TPS over time?
- How do the differences affect outcomes?
- What is the impact on business results and on people?
- What should you do if your Lean efforts don't produce significant business results?
- Toyota does not practice Lean. Why?
- TPS represents actual business needs that are common among most businesses, while Lean does not necessarily reflect actual business needs (for example: Maximize Customer Value, Perfect Processes, and Perfect Value). Does Lean reflect your actual business needs?

So, when you hear things like "Toyota is the foremost practitioner of Lean" or "Toyota, the leading lean exemplar in the world" [6], you know is it not true. You know that Lean hitched itself to Toyota to gain a free ride off of its success. In addition, the Lean Enterprise Institute (LEI) and Lean

Enterprise Academy (LEA) have been very successful at recruiting former Toyota employees to lend great credibility and legitimacy to the impression that Lean is the same as TPS.

Let's return to our inequalities:

Toyota Production System ≠ Lean Production
Toyota Management System ≠ Lean Management
Toyota Way ≠ Lean Way
Toyota Thinking ≠ Lean Thinking
Kaizen Thinking ≠ Lean Thinking
Toyota Leadership ≠ Lean Leadership
Etc.

What are the answers to the six questions?

1. How flawed is Lean?
   - It is significantly flawed.
2. How serious are the flaws?
   - They are serious.
3. Can the flaws be corrected?
   - Yes.
4. Will corrections be effective?
   - Maybe.
5. Can good things be achieved despite the flaws?
   - Yes. But the extent of good things that can be achieved is bounded by its flaws and the effectiveness of any corrections.
6. Is Lean beyond repair?
   - Maybe. If flaws go uncorrected, or if the corrections are ineffective, it is probably beyond repair.

Here is another question: Who should fix Lean?

Lean's producers should fix Lean; they should improve the product that they designed and launched into the market. It is clearly their responsibility. But, perhaps you should not rely on them to fix Lean because for nearly 30 years they have been inattentive to the flaws, either ignoring them or recognizing them decades later, despite an abundance of feedback and new information.

So, instead, you will have to fix Lean yourself in your own organization. This critique can help you do that.

1

Failure to Learn from the Past

Professor Monden's Work Ignored

Seven years before James P. Womack and Daniel T. Jones helped give us the popular version of Toyota's production system (TPS), "Lean production," there was a professor in Japan seeking to carefully understand and document in detail Toyota's production system and their overall management system. That professor was Yasuhiro Monden.

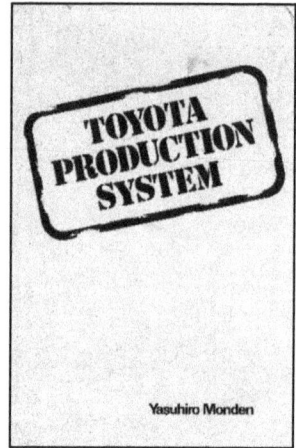

TOYOTA PRODUCTION SYSTEM

Yasuhiro Monden

Professor Monden gave us the first detailed understanding of TPS, beginning with his 1983 book, *Toyota Production System: Practical Approach to Production Management* [1]. The Foreword to the first edition was written by Taiichi Ohno. It is only a little more than one page. But, as always, Mr. Ohno has interesting things to say, some of which is repeated here because people have lost sight of the purpose, goals, methods, and way of thinking of TPS (inclusive of The Toyota Way).

In the Foreword, Mr. Ohno said [2]:

> "The technique we call Toyota production system was born… without the benefit of funds or splendid facilities."

In other words, they had to use their brains, not money.

> "Above all, one of our most important purposes was increased productivity and reduced costs."

Toyota operated in a competitive marketplace and had visions of domestic and global growth that drove the need to increase productivity and reduce costs. By costs, Ohno means all costs, not just manufacturing costs; all costs past, present, and future. When Ohno says "reduce costs," he means doing that in ways that do not harm people (non-zero-sum), especially employees. Ohno goes on to say:

"Our approach has been to investigate one by one the causes of various 'unnecessaries' in manufacturing operations and to devise methods for their solution, often by trial and error."

Most people would consider investigating, one by one, the causes of various "unnecessaries" by trial-and-error too tedious, too time-consuming, and too expensive. Instead, they would apply the same old solutions to recurring problems, whose causes remain unclear, using whatever tools or methods are at hand – and achieve only limited results.

"…it was our observation that even in Japan, it was difficult for the people of outside companies to understand our system; still less was it possible for foreign people to understand it."

Most followers of Lean are – including its producers, Womack and Jones – foreign people. Has the necessary daily study, experimentation, and practice been made to understand TPS? The answer for the vast majority of people, if they are honest, is "no."

Based upon interactions with Taiichi Ohno and others at Toyota, Professor Monden interpreted TPS this way [3]:

"…although cost-reduction is the system's most important goal, it must achieve three other sub-goals in order to achieve its primary objective. They include:

1. Quantity control, which enables the system to adapt to daily and monthly fluctuations in demand in terms of quantities and variety;

2. Quality assurance, which assures that each process will supply only good units to subsequent processes;

3. Respect-for-humanity, which must be cultivated while the system utilizes the human resources to obtain its cost objectives.

It should be emphasized here that these three goals cannot exist independently or be achieved independently without influencing each other or the primary goal of cost reduction. It is a special feature of the Toyota production system that the primary goal cannot be achieved without realization of the subgoals and vice versa. All goals are outputs of the same system; with productivity as the ultimate purpose and guiding concept, the Toyota production system strives to realize each of the goals for which it has been designed."

This is a dramatically different interpretation of TPS compared to Lean [4] (see page four). Monden's interpretation is accurate, while Lean is obviously inaccurate and thus contains many conspicuous defects.

Questions to consider:

- Why was this critically important information from 1983, in English, ignored when Lean emerged in 1988 and for all years thereafter?
- Why is the Lean interpretation of TPS so different?
- How has this difference affected people's efforts to model themselves after Toyota for the last 30 years?
- What have been the major misses in Lean transformations with respect to Professor Monden's interpretation of TPS?

Shingijutsu TPS Training

In 1988, at the dawn of the Lean era, The Kaizen Institute of America held a very important seminar on the Toyota Production System and kaizen at The Hartford Graduate Center (currently known as "Rensselaer at Hartford") in Hartford, Connecticut.

Among the attendees were representatives of Danaher Corporation, which earned notice in subsequent years for their success with the Toyota Production System (TPS). They included: George Koenigsaecker (president) and Bob Pentland (vice president) of Jacobs Manufacturing Company, and John Cosentino and Art Byrne who were Danaher group executives (Byrne would later become president and CEO of The Wiremold Company). These executives, and many other Danaher alumni, would go to lead Lean transformation in dozens of other organizations across the United States and around the world.

The featured speakers for the main seminar were Masaaki Imai (founder of the Kaizen Institute), Yoshiki Iwata, Chihiro Nakao, and Akiro Takenaka of Shingijutsu Co., Ltd. Mssrs. Iwata (d. 2001) and Nakao were former managers at Toyota subsidiaries, while Mr. Takenaka was a former production engineer. Iwata, Nakao, and Takenaka were affiliated with the "New Technology Institute." The name "New Technology" is the English translation of "shingijutsu." These were the famous kaizen consultants under which I and many others were trained.

The brochure listed the content of the seminars:

- Program A seminar "JIT/Toyota Production System"
- Program B seminar "JIT/Toyota Production System Plus In-Plant Training Exercise"
- Program C seminar "Basics of Kaizen"

The KAIZEN® Institute of America

presents

JIT/Toyota Production System Seminar
May 2-3, 1988

JIT/Toyota Production System Seminar
Plus
In-Plant Training Experience
May 2-7, 1988

Basics of KAIZEN® Seminar
May 9-10, 1988

At the
Hartford Graduate Center
Hartford, Connecticut
hosts and co-sponsors

The Kaizen Institute mistakenly linked just-in-time (JIT) and TPS in a way that implies sameness, but they are not. JIT is one of two pillar of TPS. The second pillar is jidoka (autonomation).

Key parts of the training materials reflect Toyota training materials from around 1985 or 1986. They present both a systems view and a drill-down into the tools and methods that make up TPS.

Absent were things that Lean considers to be a very important part of training, value stream maps and A3 reports, neither of which are necessary to understand abnormal conditions and improve material and information flow. Finally, the training emphasized the importance of management involvement in TPS, which remains a major struggle today for Lean.

Page one of the "JIT/Toyota Production System" seminar says:

> "Basic Concept (Roles of Manufacturing Department in the age of limited-quantity production)."

The term "limited-quantity production" means that markets have shifted from sellers' (supply-driven; produce as many as one can make) to buyers' (demand-driven; produce only as many as can be sold). Recognizing TPS as a management system designed for buyers' markets, and its disdain for economies of scale (for fear of overproduction), are critical points that most people today still fail to grasp.

Iwata's training session begins with the words:

> "Building GEMBA strong enough to cope with change: The Challenge to Flow Production."

Building the gemba (correct spelling is "genba") means building the capabilities of the workforce to recognize abnormal conditions (e.g. queues) and eliminating them via kaizen. Specifically, Toyota's industrial engineering-based kaizen method, whose focus is eliminating waste through constant trail-and-error.

These seminars would be repeated over the next few years due to the high concentration of manufacturing businesses in the greater Hartford, Connecticut area. Additional seminars topics included Total Quality Management (TQM) and Quality Function Deployment (QFD). This represents just the beginning of what one needs to know to successfully introduce TPS to an organization.

Shingijutsu [5] helped bring TPS to America and made a positive impact on many organizations [6]. The companies that hired Shingijutsu and received training in Toyota's industrial engineering-based kaizen method typically prospered to a far greater extent that those who used other consultants whose focus was Lean, not TPS.

Herein lies the significance of Shingijutsu's work. They were the first former Toyota engineers to teach TPS to others using kaizen as the principal teaching method. These former Toyota employees, with 30 years of TPS experience, though the thing that their clients need to know most was Toyota's industrial engineering-based kaizen method. In addition, kaizen served as a method to promote teamwork, individual development, organizational development, and leadership development. And kaizen is the principal method for achieving cost reduction and productivity improvement in ways that do not harm people (e.g. employees).

What business does not benefit from cost reduction and productivity improvement if it can be achieved in a non-zero-sum way? Toyota's industrial engineering-based kaizen method is the key.

With Lean, Toyota's kaizen method is an afterthought. For many years, the emphasis was on teaching people tools extracted from kaizen, such as value stream maps, A3 reports, 5S, visual controls and so on, in a classroom setting. These tools have served mainly as a method to promote individual development. And, unfortunately, Lean is often associated with improvement that results in harm to people (e.g. employee layoffs due to process improvement).

Again, we see a major difference between TPS and Lean: How people are trained and what people are trained in. While the use of tools extracted from kaizen can result in meaningful improvement, the magnitude of improvement is small compared to what can be achieved using kaizen.

Questions to consider:

- Why didn't the producers of Lean grasp the significance of Toyota's industrial engineering-based kaizen method early-on (late-1980s)?
- Why has kaizen remained a minor feature in Lean for the last 30 years?
- How much cost reduction can be achieved without kaizen?
- How much productivity improvement can be achieved without kaizen?
- Is the actual target customer/market for Lean those organizations that don't want (or think they don't need) kaizen?
- Is Toyota's kaizen method not used by organizations that have adopted Lean because it reduces management control and places too much power in the hands of workers?

Lean Did Not Learn from History

The history of modern industrial management begins with Scientific Management. It informed the development and evolution of Toyota's production system and its derivative, "Lean production." This includes the life and times of Frederick Winslow Taylor (1856-1915), the father of Scientific Management [7, 8], as well as the work of The Taylor Society which was formed after Taylor's death in 1915 to further advance Scientific Management.

Study of the evolution of Scientific Management between 1890 to the late 1920s reveals much about the challenges that the Lean movement has faced since its inception in 1988. Had there been awareness of this history, many mistakes and frustrations might have been avoided.

The Scientific Management movement encountered numerous barriers and its leaders faced constant challenges from business leaders and society. Most of their experiences will be familiar to the proponents of Lean, and therein lies a major problem: Not learning from history.

- The leaders of Scientific Management were overconfident in their aims and their ability to influence business leaders. While important innovations in management were made (and critical to the success of wartime efforts), many of which remain with us today, the Scientific Management movement's success relative to its expansive vision was far less than Taylor and his followers had hoped for.

- The Scientific Management community was both part of business yet separate from it. They operated at levels below the C-suite, and were never able to become fully part of the executive office, except for in a hand full of cases.

- Within companies, Scientific Management engineers did not / could not / were not allowed to cross boundaries into the top levels of corporate leadership and influence its policies, thought processes, strategies, or decisions. Scientific Management practitioners were of a different rank – a lower order – than the executive, despite their view of themselves as right in matters of fact and more capable of business leadership.

- Engineers became seen by CEOs as insufficiently motivated by profits to lead, while engineers saw CEOs as too tainted by the profit motive (and the "cesspool of commercialism") to understand and embrace Scientific Management.

- To help gain a wider audience, Scientific Management orthodoxies were eventually loosened. In contemporary terms, inclusion of six-sigma, change management, and similar things have been permitted entry or welcomed into Lean management.

- In the vast majority of cases, the audience for Scientific Management had no interest in and (being a lower order than the CEO) was incapable of completely changing an organization's system of management. Minor changes to the existing management system was good enough.

- The initial focus of Scientific Management on production eventually gave way to new areas of application such as Scientific Management in sales, purchasing, the office, government, the home, and so on.

- Scientific Management, developed to serve sellers' markets, had difficulty adjusting to the emergence of buyers' markets staring around the mid-1920s. Toyota (specifically, Taiichi Ohno *et al.*) solved this problem some 35 years later.

- The early focus on individuals and centralization of authority for work evolved into a focus on groups, teamwork, and more decentralized authority for how to do the job. In contemporary terms, the focus on teamwork has given way to a focus on individuals; e.g. coaching kata.

- The emphasis on "money-making" possessed by the CEO was seen as evidence for the need to transform business into a profession through the development of "technical knowledge, training, and discipline" which Scientific Management could bring, therefore resulting in competent and dignified leadership. The same need for professionalism exists today in both management and leadership.

- The profit motive was a "controlling influence" on the CEO. That, in addition to corporate survival and market dominance meant that Scientific Management would never be influential with the CEO rank despite its potential to deliver greater profits. The same situation exists today, with additional need to accumulate vast personal wealth.

- In its day, Scientific Management greatly influenced the thinking of progressive social and political leaders, and vice versa. Little or no such influence among social or political leaders existed between 1985 to 2017 for Lean.

- The engineer's facts (from time studies and other industrial engineering methods) could not overcome the subjective opinions of leaders (CEO rank) or their corporate economic, social, or political interests. They could not get top leaders to see work scientifically.

- In large organizations, the middle management problem – resistance to change – went uncorrected because its causes were not well understood. This problem exists today, though its source is well understood [9].

- With few exceptions, CEOs and CFOs were unable to grasp how wages for workers could be high while simultaneously having low costs. This remains true today, despite the "professionalization" of management via business school education.

- With few exceptions, workers resisted Scientific Management because they did not believe high wages would be forthcoming, or that higher wages would not be arbitrarily cut by management. To the CEOs, high wages as perceived simply as higher labor costs, while higher productivity was seen as something they could get for market (or lower) wages and through the introduction of new labor-saving technologies.

- Workers and labor unions were also concerned that Scientific Management would bring about diminution of skills and loss of control over the work. These concerns remain with us today, within or outside the context of organized labor.

- Neither Taylor nor the aims of Scientific Management were hostile to labor unions. The view was simply that unions were unnecessary because management would fully satisfy workers' financial and other needs in those companies where Scientific Management was "installed." Later, Scientific Management leaders came to accept collective bargaining as necessary response to exploitative industrial conditions. Labor unions would eventually ally with Scientific Management because it was seen as a way to strengthen unions and maintain higher wages for workers.

- CEOs preferred to spend money on productivity-improving technologies and equipment versus improving work processes. To them, the former was recognized as a sure thing, while benefits from the latter were uncertain. This remains true today as well.

- The new field of management consulting consisted of a small group of consultants faithful to Scientific Management and Taylor's orthodoxy, and a horde of consultants who claimed to be experts in Scientific Management but who immediately diluted Taylor's orthodoxy and made use of any device or method that improved efficiency. This created great confusion in the marketplace over what Scientific management was or was not. The "charlatans" were far more successful than the management consultants who faithfully adhered to Taylor's orthodoxy.

Ultimately, Scientific Management did not do enough for workers in terms of improved pay and working conditions, principally due to misunderstanding and malpractice by supervisors and mid-level managers. Scientific Management was unsuccessful in engaging leaders in the C-suite, whether to improve the business, professionalize business leaders, or advance its own interests.

Henry Gantt, a close associate of Frederick Winslow Taylor, had a maxim that said:

"The usual way of doing a thing is always the wrong way."

Based on the history and evolution of Scientific Management, it seems that the approach taken to advancing Lean management has been the usual way of doing a thing.

Questions to consider:

- Knowing the history of Scientific Management, which lessons should the producers of Lean have been mindful of?
- What has Lean done for workers in terms of pay and employment stability?
- How could the methods used for advancing Lean have been improved: a) at inception and b) in later years?

The Wisdom of Henry Gantt

Henry Gantt (1861-1919) was an esteemed associate of Frederick Winslow Taylor, the father of Scientific Management, which was the predecessor to TPS and Lean management. Gantt was an accomplished engineer, well-schooled in business affairs, and an astute observer of human nature. His efforts to advance Taylor's Scientific Management enjoyed some success, but he also experienced many barriers.

Gantt documented some of his experiences and observations in various books, including *Industrial Leadership*, published in 1916 [10]. Gantt wrote forthrightly about the problems with American business and American business leaders. He did not shroud his opinions in diplomacy.

Gantt's observations about business and leaders at the turn of the 20th century reveal an amazing sameness or similarity to the problems encountered today in advancing Lean management. The following excerpts from *Industrial Leadership* pertain to leadership:

> [The] natural tendency [of financiers and merchants], therefore, was to apply to the purchase of labor the same rules which they had applied to the purchase of materials, namely, to buy it as cheaply as possible. (p. 3)

In context, Gantt makes the case that labor is vastly different from material and must be carefully acquired, developed, and rewarded.

> Moreover, it is becoming recognized that the good man at high wages not only does more work per dollar of wages than the poor man at low wages, but better work... the policy of paying satisfactory wages has been more influential in low costs than any other item. (p. 7)

Managers today still think that low wages equals low costs, and high wages equals high costs. What accounts for such ignorance?

> If there is any one principle, which more than any other, is influential in promoting the success of an organization, it is the following: *The authority to issue an order involves the responsibility to see that it is properly executed* [italics original]. The system of management which we advocate is based on this principle, which eliminates "bluff" as a feature in management, for a man can only assume the responsibility for doing a thing properly when he not only knows how to do it, but can also teach somebody else to do it. (p. 8)

Today managers issue orders and walk away. They must instead know how to do the work.

> ...in all problems of administration the most important element is the human element, compels acceptance of the democratic idea... unless men are studied from a democratic standpoint, the student [manager] fails to get a proper appreciation of the human element. (p. 17)

People living in a democratic society want to experience the same or something close to it at work.

> Under autocratic methods to render service is a sign of inferiority; the man of power compels the service of others. Under democratic methods the man of power uses that power to serve others. (p. 19)

That should not be difficult for managers to understand, but it is.

> The industrial leader of the future must practice methods which are approved by the people, and they must be such as not to take unfair advantage of anybody. (p. 22)

Nobody wants to be the loser. Workers want non-zero-sum (win-win) outcomes.

> The general policy of the past has been to drive, but the era of force must give way to that of knowledge, and the policy of the future will be to teach and to lead, to the advantage of all concerned. (p. 25)

Managers need to understand that part of their job is to be a teacher – a good teacher.

> This brings us again to the importance of wise direction, or proper leadership. Our ideals must be correct, or our whole scheme of efficiency falls to the ground. Striving efficiently for improper ends may involve all concerned in a catastrophe, the extent of which is measured only be the efficiency with which the end has been striven for. (p. 44)

Managers' concerned with short-term gains at the expense of others possess ideals that will create bigger problems in the long-run.

> The attempt to substitute scientific knowledge for opinion in the administration of human affairs is what is known as "scientific management," which might better be called 'the scientific method in management. (p. 59)

It is remarkable how opinion continues to trump facts in the administration of human affairs in business.

> The other fallacy, viz., that it is necessary to have low wages in order to have low costs, is equally detrimental to all concerned. (p. 66)

The cause-and-effect associated with low wages has broad negative impacts, not narrow impacts as most see it.

This is a sample of Mr. Gantt's views on leadership, based on his extensive experience as a management consultant. Gantt would no doubt be upset and disappointed with today's leaders. They remain committed to the narrow view that labor can be purchased just like anything else, and have done little or nothing to democratize the workplace. They force a seemingly never-ending series of zero-sum (win-lose) outcomes on employees, from flat wages to wage cuts and benefits cuts, to achieve short-term gains for shareholders.

· · · · ·

The following excerpts pertain to financiers and accountants. Referring to financiers and merchants, Gantt said:

> Their natural tendency, therefore, was to apply to the purchase of labor the same rules which they had applied to the purchase of materials, namely, to buy it as cheaply as possible. (p. 3)

In context, Gantt makes the case that labor is vastly different from material and must be carefully acquired, developed, and rewarded. The consequences of cheap labor are undesirable for a business, and include low quality work and workers who perform only well-enough to keep their job.

> Too often the system of cost accounting has been to a large extent to blame, for the systems in general use often fail to disclose the real troubles, and content themselves with blaming the shop with inefficiency... the call for efficiency which has been so loudly proclaimed throughout the country for several years has had a great deal of influence on shop organizations, but *it has hardly been heeded at all in the financial and selling ends of the business, where it is needed even worse than in the shops.* [italics original] (pp. 38-39)

Finance departments remain notable laggards in the application of Lean to finance and accounting work.

> The cost keeping and accounting methods in general use in our industries today are so devised as to put all the blame for failure on the producing portion of the business, and do no show the loss due to improper business policies, which it is safe to say are a more fertile source of failure than the mistakes made by the production end of the business. (p. 39)

This remains true today in any organization that continues to use standard cost accounting.

> It is necessary that our cost keeping and accounting methods of the future shall show what losses are due to an unwise policy, or to poor management… or industrial scheme will not be rounded out until we have a means of measuring the ability with which those at the head of the business perform their functions, that is at least as good as that which we use to measure the efficiency of the operative. (p. 39)

We now have that means. It is called Lean accounting.

> The time will come, however, and indeed is not far distant, when cost keeping and accounting methods… will be so changed as to place blame for failure where it belongs, and give credit to whom credit is due. (p. 40)

Lean accounting will help assign problems to the correct areas so that root cause analysis can be performed in a non-blaming, non-judgmental way.

> Our difficulty in the past has been mainly with the commercial man, who has certain theories of efficiency

gained from the cost accountant which are fatal to our efforts to make improvements of any kind. (p. 65)

Indeed, the "commercial man," focused on selling, lives on, and continues to remain closely aligned with status-quo oriented cost accountants.

...the financier, in many cases, still sincerely believes the accountant to be more important than the manufacturer, even though he only keeps a record of what the manufacturer does. (p. 68)

Manufacturing is where value is created, not in accounting. The financier needs to pay attention to manufacturing.

...it is time we readjusted the traditional relative positions of the record keeper and the doer. The record keeper is just as essential as ever, but under modern methods he must yield his supremacy to the producer, and give up his privilege of being simply a critic. (p. 69)

The account must become actively engaged in continuous improvement though participation in kaizen.

This is a sample of Mr. Gantt's views on financiers and accountants. Gantt would no doubt be upset and disappointed with today's leaders for a number of reasons:

- Thinking the best way to reduce unit costs was by offshoring work to low wage countries, thereby continuing the long tradition of failing to understand the difference between unit cost and total cost.
- Driving suppliers to set up businesses in low wage countries, and then, a decade or more later, take credit for re-shoring work back to the United States (e.g. Walmart, General Electric).

- Extending payment terms to supplies, which, in effect, raises their costs. But, unable to pass the increased costs on to their customers, suppliers suffer reduced profits which threaten the future existence of their business.
- Harming suppliers' interests instead of helping them improve their processes.
- Reflexively adopting technology to replace labor.
- Remaining more adept at speculation and exploiting resources than improving the processes used to create value
  for customers.
- Hoarding cash, thereby reducing business investment.
- Cutting employee wages and benefits.

Ultimately, Gantt would be upset that, 100 years later, the pinnacle of management practice remains zero-sum. He would be disappointed in leaders for not evolving towards non-zero-sum business practices, and disappointed in government and society for not holding business leaders accountable.

Questions to consider:

- Why are we experiencing the same problems in 2017 as Gantt experienced in 1900?
- Why hasn't the mindset or thinking of business leaders advanced?
- Why is business decision-making largely the same for 100-plus years?
- Why don't business leaders eagerly embrace Lean management?
- What role, if any, do business schools play in perpetuating the status quo of conventional management thinking and practice?

Historical Parallels

Historical parallels are never exact. But, they are often similar enough to one another in circumstances and outcomes that the parallels can be striking. Such is the case between Scientific Management 100 years ago and Lean management today. We begin with Scientific Management.

While Frederick Winslow Taylor is acknowledged as the creator of Scientific Management, he did not do his revolutionary work alone. There were others who worked closely with him and had important roles to play, including Carl Barth, Morris Cooke, Henry Gantt, and Horace Hathaway. Others worked with Taylor but also did their own unique work contemporaneously, such as Frank and Lillian Gilbreth. This was a cadre of several men and one woman who set out to make change for the better.

Along with Taylor were some academics, working in the new field of industrial administration. These included Horace Drury, Henry Farquhar, Harlow Person, and C. Bertrand Thompson. As might be expected, some academics studied Scientific Management closely while a few also had actual industrial work experience. Those with work experience were better able to understand the technical, human, business, and economic intent of Scientific Management. Other academics lacking such experience tended to be critical of Scientific Management – especially those academics after World War II, primarily due to terrible ex-post facto analysis of Taylor's work.

Scientific Management, also known as "The Taylor System" was a fragile system of management. It could only be applied in its entirety, in a precise way, in order to assure its success. Under the skilled care of Taylor and his associates, several manufacturing and a few service firms succeeded in achieving the major aims of Scientific Management, which was to increase output and profits for the business, increase productivity, reduce costs, simplify work, and substantially increase the pay of workers.

To achieve that result, Taylor's associates adhered to all four of Taylor's principles and the many associated practices, and they worked hard to ensure that the management of the organizations they consulted with were fully committed in order to achieve good results and avoid negative backlash or failure.

Because it was a fragile management system, most people could not "install" Scientific Management. Yet, as Scientific Management was revolutionary, many people flocked to it to become consultants. They learned enough about it, usually by reading books or magazine articles, and picked out the parts they liked the best. They would then install something similar in appearance to Scientific Management in organizations whose leaders did not comprehend the consultants' lack of knowledge and experience. They named themselves "efficiency engineers," and soon a large and influential "efficiency movement" was born. These people were very successful at exploiting Scientific Management and unsuspecting business owners. Taylorists referred to these people as "fakirs" and "charlatans."

Taylor and his associates had disdain for efficiency engineers and the efficiency movement because Scientific Management was much more than just efficiency, worthy as that is. Its objectives were to improve the strength of American industry, eliminate disputes between labor and management, create high-quality repeatable processes, reduce costs, improve corporate profitability, improve productivity, improve working conditions, increase workers' pay, and so on.

Taylor and his associates also wanted to teach business leaders that high wages were a sure path to low costs, and break manager's habit of cutting workers' pay in the mistaken beliefs that it reduces costs. Taylor and his associates knew that the work performed by the "fakirs" and "charlatans" would lead to poor outcomes for the company and its workers, as well as its customers. And that was what indeed happened. Yet, efficiency engineers – some of whom were former academics or know-nothing job seekers who had little actual business experience – became popular and far more financially successful that Taylor's cadre of intelligent and experienced management consultants.

In testimony to Congress in 1912 [8], Taylor said:

> "It ceases to be scientific management the
> moment it is used for bad."

From experience, Taylor knew that Scientific Management must do no harm. Taylor developed his system with the expressed intent to improve management practice, not to do harm and worsen management practice. Scientific management, installed in a precise way, did not harm employees, but efficiency engineers and the efficiency movement did. That is because the efficiency engineers did not care about and did not install Scientific Management. They installed other things – dilutions of Scientific Management – that invariably led to layoffs and other short-term gains for their clients.

Taylor's work – application of the scientific method to management and the creation of industrial engineering – had a profound influence on the development of Toyota's production system and overall management practice. That would not be the case for Lean upon its emergence in 1988 and thereafter.

· · · · ·

In the early 1970s, soon after the oil shocks, people both inside and outside of Japan started to become aware of Toyota's production system and began to study it. Wonderful work was done by Kiyoshi Suzaki, Richard Schonberger, Yasuhiro Monden, Robert Hall, Masaaki Imai, and others to understand TPS. The books and papers they wrote generated a lot of interest in Toyota's methods. It is noteworthy that most – but not all – of the early study of TPS was its technical aspects, not its human aspects. When the human aspects were described, it was usually both limited in scope and brief in explanation.

Like Taylor, Taiichi Ohno did not do his revolutionary work alone. There were many others who worked closely with him and had important roles to play, including Yukio Arima, Kikuo Suzumura, Fujio Cho, and Chihiro Nakao. While Taylor's approach to improvement was more purely science- and engineering-based, Ohno-san's approach to improvement was different. It was a combination of engineer (scientific method) and mechanic (trial-and-error). In general, the scientific method was used for problem identification (observation, question, hypothesis) while extensive trial-and-error (experiments, validate/refute hypothesis, repeat) resulted in problem-solving and learning.

The Toyota's production system's principles, Just-in-Time and Jidoka (autonomation), were extensively studied and presented in books, conference presentations, and so on. Yet, consultants and managers would "implement" (not "install") only just-in-time and forget about jidoka and everything else that made TPS function correctly. Managers wanted the cost savings that would result from pushing their massive inventories upstream to suppliers, but without making any fundamental changes to their own processes. Kanban, a method for achieving just-in-time, became something of interest as well, though largely separated from the rest of TPS.

From the late 1970s through the late 1980s, a small army of consultants sold business leaders on JIT, kanban, and other "tools" of TPS. There was a ready market for that in the

United States and elsewhere as global competition began to intensify in certain industries. Ohno-san and his cadre of Toyota associates surely viewed such consultants as "fakirs" and "charlatans." But this bad situation was soon to get much worse.

In the mid-1980s, researchers at the Massachusetts Institute of Technology begin to study Toyota's Production System. To a great extent, the study of TPS was performed by academics, though some of the graduate students had industry experience. In 1988, the term "Lean production" is presented to the world as a synonymous or generic term for TPS, and was understood narrowly as a "production system" – not as an overall management system as Ohno-san had thought it to be. So TPS was seen as beneficial for operations, but not for any other part of the business such as purchasing, IT, human resources, engineering, etc. Yet, fundamentally, TPS was Toyota's management system.

In addition, TPS, the creation of which is suffused with Japanese thinking and context, was, as discussed earlier, studied by English speaking people – though there were some exceptions; e.g. Takahiro Fujimoto, Toshihiro Nishiguchi. Despite this, researchers missed many important nuances and details. That missing information led to major problems with Lean transformations, such that most efforts were unsuccessful. Contrast that with Scientific Management, where there were no translation problems. Yet, people still had great difficulty understanding it. And the "fakirs" and "charlatans" were ever-present then, as now.

Soon, the "Lean movement" was born and the term "continuous improvement engineer" later became common. It spawned an army of consultants – a huge army of consultants – most of whom had little actual experience with TPS. They understood the technical and business aspects of TPS, but few understood the human aspects of Toyota management. Failure to understand the human aspects led to Fake Scientific Management then, just as it did Fake Lean management today (defined as "Continuous Improvement" only, no "Respect for People").

Ohno-san and other who had deep knowledge of TPS surely knew the "fakirs" and "charlatans" had no choice but to leave out various important elements because they had no experience creating TPS. In 1978, Ono said: "…those who decide to implement the Toyota production system must be fully committed. If you try to adopt only the 'good parts', you'll fail" [11]. Lean management, representing a severe dilution of Toyota Management (i.e. "the good parts"), combined with its "fakir" and "charlatan" consultants meant that failure was inevitable for most organizations.

In 2001, Toyota published "The Toyota Way 2001" [12], in which it explicitly articulated "Continuous Improvement" and "Respect for People" as the two pillars of The Toyota Way. Toyota made explicit what had long been implicit: People are central to the achievement of continuous improvement. To that end, people must be allowed to think and given opportunities every day to contribute to making their job easier while achieving better results. The importance of respecting people – all stakeholders; employees, suppliers, customers, investors, and communities – was something that had long been apparent if one had closely read various works written by Toyota leaders and others, including their speeches and news stories, as well as the history of Scientific Management.

After a lag of six or seven years, the producers of the Lean movement finally recognized the "Respect for People" principle [13], something that Taylor had fought for over 100 years ago (called "cooperation" in his day). Lean practitioners began to realize that Lean transformations were failing because management did not respect people and were laying them off after improvements had been made. Not only were organizations failing to "become Lean," few, if any, had even come close to what Toyota achieved in the 25 years after World War II.

It ceases to be Lean management the moment it is used for bad. Harming people does not respect people. These were the same problems that plagued Scientific Management more than 100 years ago, leading to the same six criticisms from workers.

There seems to have been a failure among the MIT researchers pre-1988 and Womack and Jones post-1988 to accurately comprehend TPS as well as the history Scientific Management and industrial engineering, and thinking that TPS was something entirely different from Scientific Management, when, in fact, Scientific Management and TPS (Toyota Management) are closely related from both technical and human perspectives.

In 2007, the term "lean production" was replaced with "Lean management." The Lean movement readily adopted the term Lean management because the term Lean production had become worn out over the prior 20 years and also apparently reflected new learning on the part of those who produced Lean.

There is no doubt that Ohno-san (were he alive) and his Toyota associates would have disdain for today's continuous improvement engineers, akin to yesterday's "efficiency engineers" and the Lean movement because Toyota Management, like Scientific Management, is about more than just continuous improvement – or wealth creation, growth, or competitive advantage – worthy as those are. Its objectives are much   more expansive and also fundamental to corporate survival and deeply intertwined with developing people and the betterment of humanity.

What has happened over the last 100-plus years is more than just a curiosity, and the practical consequences have been significant. Efforts made by a great many people over long periods of time to improve the practice of management have produced limited business results. The common consequence of Lean remains: Employees are in various ways harmed by Lean. Suppliers and customers often don't fare much better.

Questions to consider:

- Why did it take the producers of the Lean movement seven years after They Toyota Way 2001 was published to begin to recognize the "Respect for People" principle?
- Why did it take 20 years to replace the term "lean production" with "Lean management?"
- What are the responsibilities of the owners of a movement to its followers and other stakeholders?
- Would knowing the true nature of Scientific Management and its challenges have made a difference in how Lean was understood by researchers and practiced by managers?
- Would knowing the true nature of Toyota management earlier in the Lean movement have made a difference in how Lean was understood and practiced?
- Would more business leaders have listened and made things better for employees, suppliers, customers, investors, and communities if Lean was actually the same as TPS?

Same Six Criticisms from Workers

Ever since the beginning of progressive management*, starting with Scientific Management in the late 1800s and all the way to Lean management today, workers have had the same six criticisms. In their view, progressive management is bad because it will:

- De-humanize me
- Speed me up and burn me out
- De-skill me
- Take away my knowledge
- Take away my creativity
- Cost me my job

This is an almost universal reaction among workers, whether they are laborers or professionals – sometimes even before they have learned anything about progressive management.

The default viewpoint among workers is that management always seeks to do harm to them, both professionally and personally. That is a heavy burden for management to bear, and one which impedes efforts to improve management practice. Why do workers think this way about managers?

Workers reasons to fear progressive management are sound because, more likely than not, their leaders do not understand it at all and because they will ignore the "Respect for People" principle. Most leaders think progressive management is a more effective way to cut costs, especially by laying people after improvements have been made.

---

* "Progressive management" is an umbrella term used throughout this book to describe the principal types of progressive management that have emerged over time: Scientific Management, Toyota Production System and The Toyota Way, and Lean management.

Recall Toyota's motivation for creating TPS: Cost reduction and productivity improvement in order to satisfy customers and survive. In other words, motivation for creating TPS was to grown and improve, and to do so in ways that did not cause harm to the employees or to any of its stakeholders (suppliers, customers, investors, and communities). Toyota leaders recognized that people's ideas and creativity were necessary in order to achieve material and information flow. If harm is done to employees, then flow will never be created.

This is the weakness of Lean: People are harmed, and so flow is never created. No flow means that costs will remain high and productivity will not be significantly improved. The decades-long absence of "Respect for People" in Lean means that harm could be done to people – employees and other stakeholders – as a result of continuous improvement alone. The widespread existence of Fake Lean since the inception of Lean in 1988 confirms that harm was indeed done.

Reality informs us, without any difficulty, that nobody wants to be the loser. Therefore, management should not make people, especially employees, the loser. But, most managers do not know how to achieve improved business results without making someone the loser. And, Lean does not teach them how to improve in ways that do not make losers. Only TPS does that.

When business leaders make employees the loser, efforts to create a Lean organization will obviously fail. This should be easy to understand, but it is not given the deeply ingrained patterns of management thinking and decision-making. If managers want all the benefits of TPS, then they must practice TPS, not Lean. Practicing TPS will help them eliminate the six criticisms of Lean.

Leaders of the Lean movement have recently made efforts to help managers gain a better understanding of the purpose and intent of Lean management, and the importance of "Respect for People." However, the only way for managers to develop an understanding of "Respect for People" and its many connections to "Continuous Improvement" is through personal engagement in kaizen. It cannot be achieved through classroom training or a one-day executive workshop.

Management participation in kaizen will demonstrate to employees that Lean is being used to grow and improve, not to cause harm to employees. Employees need to see tangible evidence of non-zero-sum outcomes to prove that Lean is beneficial to them, as well as to other stakeholders.

Any employee who has experienced TPS, knows that it:

- Humanizes the workplace and improves cooperation, communication, and enthusiasm for work
- Focuses and energizes
- Adds skills to one's repertoire
- Increases knowledge
- Increases creativity
- Makes the job more valuable and secure

In the vast majority of cases, these are not the cluster of employee outcomes associated with Lean.

Questions to consider:

- Why do managers think doing harm to people is an acceptable management practice?
- Is it the job of managers to do harm to people in the fulfillment of their responsibilities?
- Why are zero-sum outcomes so common in organizations?

- What level of management skill and capability is required to achieve zero-sum outcomes compared to non-zero-sum outcomes?
- Why don't the leading business schools teach non-zero-sum management (i.e. TPS)?
- How does the need for survival, or not, affect management zero-sum/non-zero-sum thinking and decision-making?

History Matters

Most people who are interested in Toyota's management practice have no interest in the history of progressive management and ideas that led to its creation. Nor is there much interest in the problems and difficulties faced by those who worked to advance progressive management prior to TPS. The lack of curiosity unfortunate given that Lean people claim a devotion to learning, which is initiated through curiosity.

People think that what they see today represents the good stuff because all the bad stuff was filtered out in the decades prior. Surely smart people in years gone by would not carry forward bad ways of thinking and doing things, right? That is a flawed assumption.

If we do not understand this as fact, then we cannot move past the many bad ways of thinking and doing things remain with us today. History helps make this clear and imbues us with wisdom to avoid repeating mistakes that harm people and which consume precious resources such as time, material, money, and human energy.

People should want to learn the history of progressive management so that we can answer important questions such as:

1. What immediately preceded the creation of Toyota's production system?
2. What were the assumptions and business needs that led to the creation of progressive management practice?
3. How did the creators of progressive management put their new ideas into practice?
4. What kinds of problems did they face in advancing the new management practice?
5. How influential were early progressive management ideas and practices in the creation of TPS?

6. Why do business leaders struggle so much to understand progressive management?

7. What effective countermeasures can be applied to overcome leaders' resistance to progressive management?

8. How can progressive management be so popular with some people, yet simultaneously so unpopular with other people? Why do such divergent views exist and persist?

Answering these questions about the past, as well as surrounding factors such as economics, politics, and social hierarchies, helps us better understand the current condition and future state of Lean. Will Lean continue to thrive? Will it maintain its current level of popularity? Will Lean die quickly or fade away slowly? What factors contribute to its continuation, growth, or demise? These are questions whose answers may lie in the past, and so we should study it so that we can learn from it.

Another important question is why the creators of Lean have been so disinterested in gaining an accurate understanding of the history of progressive management between the years 1880 to 1935. It is a heritage that they work very hard to disassociate from Lean. The better approach would have been to confront the past and teach people how Scientific Management informed the development of TPS and the derivative work called "Lean." Doing so might have improved how Lean was seen by people and resulted in broader acceptance – especially among workers. Instead, the intelligent and thoughtful work of the truly innovative management pioneers who came before TPS has been ignored or misinterpreted.

It is remarkable that the good people who brought us Lean, Womack and Jones, could so easily fall prey to, and perpetuate, the common view that those who created the antecedent to TPS were villains, rather than, as scholars, seek the facts to understand the important work done a century ago, its evolution, and how it continues to be part of Toyota's management practice today.

One of the things that they would soon realize is that Scientific Management circa 1912 is better aligned with TPS and the Toyota Way than Lean was when it was introduced to the public in 1988 and for nearly decades thereafter. The numerous points of alignment are shown in the table below:

Scientific Management (ca. 1912)	Toyota Management
Application of Scientific Method to management	Application of Scientific Method to management
Required change for managers and workers: Mental Revolution	Required change for managers and workers: Cognitive Revolution
System to learn better methods	System to learn better methods
Method of improvement: Industrial Engineering tools	Method of improvement: Industrial Engineering tools + others
Specialization in work performed	Specialization in work performed
Knowledge-based processing controlled by management	Knowledge-based processing controlled by workers and management
Facts derived from science, observation	Fact-based, go see
Improvement by observation and experimentation	Improvement by observation and rapid experimentation
Scientific selection of workers	Careful selection of workers
Scientifically trained workers	Scientifically trained workers (kaizen)
Cooperation and trust between management and workers	Cooperation and trust between management and workers
Technical Focus: Betterment	Technical Focus: Continuous Improvement
Human Focus: Cooperation	Human Focus: Respect for People
Business Focus: Improve operations processes	Business Focus: Improve all processes
A corporate strategy? No	A corporate strategy? No.

The key figures leading the Scientific Management movement were intelligent, deeply thoughtful people, with good intentions, who dedicated their lives to improving American industrial strength, the practice of management, and life for workers both on- and off-the-job. Frederick Winslow Taylor *et al.* are not the horrible villains that they have been made out to be.

Below are four impressive works that are well worth reading. The first is a 13-page paper by Morris Cooke that succinctly illuminates the intent of Scientific Management, which is to benefit both owners and workers. Next is a powerful essay by Horace King Hathaway which every Lean practitioner can relate to. Finally, two powerful books by Frank and Lillian Gilbreth that provide important details about Scientific Management from both technical and human perspectives.

- "The Spirit and Social Significance of Scientific Management," Morris Cooke, *The Journal of Political Economy*, Vol. 21, No. 6, June 1913
- "The Men Who Succeed in Scientific Management," H.K. Hathaway (pages 46-54), in *A Symposium on Scientific Management and Efficiency in College Education*, 1913. The Papers Presented at the Efficiency Session of the Twelfth Annual Convention of the Society for the Promotion of Engineering Education, Boston, Mass., 26-29 June 1912
- *Primer of Scientific Management,* Frank Gilbreth, D. Van Nostrand Co., New York, NY, 1914
- *The Psychology of Management*, Lillian Gilbreth, Sturgis and Walton Co., New York, NY, 1914

Questions to consider:

- Does separating Lean from Scientific Management achieve the intended outcome of alleviating criticism of Lean by workers?
- A fundamental practice when conducting research is to give credit where credit is due. Why do the originators of Lean fail in this important responsibility?
- Is it good research practice to approve of one body of information and ignore or mischaracterize another body of information?
- Should researchers ignore work done long ago because it does not conform to the context of the present day?

2

Poor Interpretation of TPS

No "Respect for People"

There is a great mystery surrounding the emergence and subsequent promotion of "lean production" beginning in 1988. It is the absence of "Respect for People" for nearly 20 years. "Respect for People" was long part of the Toyota Production System (TPS) and a prominent feature of progressive management before that. So why wasn't it part of lean production?

While Womack and Jones have long been the principals leading efforts to promote Lean, other organizations, such as the Association for Manufacturing Excellence, and the Shingo Institute, also did not recognize "Respect for People" as a requirement for the practice of Toyota-like progressive management. Many others missed it as well, both academics and practitioners – though there were some notable exceptions [1].

The awakening finally began in 2008 – an amazing lag of seven years after Toyota published The Toyota Way 2001 internal document [2] – but it did not become a force until after 2010, and especially after 2014. Why then?

In my own experience with TPS beginning in 1994, I found the need to respect people as obvious almost from the start, in part simply by recognizing that workers will not participate in kaizen if it costs them their job. Also, sensei from Shingijutsu taught us, on day 1, the importance of respecting people because workers are the wellspring of creative ideas and improvement action.

My understanding of "Respect for People" has evolved greatly over time and has been central to my work and to my understanding of continuous improvement and flow. I soon recognized the need for a different approach to leadership, one that respected people and which results in improved creativity and information flow. Remarkably, "Lean leadership" did not become a specific item of interest within the Lean community until 2007.

Both Womack and Jones should have learned about "Respect for People" from numerous sources:

- Time spent with Shingijutsu sensei in the early 1990s
- While conducting research for the books *The Machine that Changed the World* and *Lean Thinking* [3, 4]
- The first book on TPS by Yasuhiro Monden [5]
- Dozens of Toyota and NUMMI executives and managers that they interviewed
- Their MIT research associate, John Krafcik, the former NUMMI employee who coined the term "lean" [6]
- Their close colleague John Shook, a Toyota and NUMMI veteran
- A noteworthy journal paper written by Toyota engineers [7]
- Dozens of speeches by Toyota leaders over the decades
- A 1991 document from a NUMMI employee that contrasted GM and Toyota beliefs and values, and which highlighted the importance of "Respect for People" [8]
- Careful study of Scientific Management and the subsequent evolution of progressive management post-Taylor

The information, in one form or another, has long been in existence.

Importantly, any talk of flow that is absent "Respect for People" is akin to trying to make bread without water. It is a major error both in understanding of TPS and in promoting Lean to think that flow can be achieved without "Respect for

People." Flow cannot be disconnected from "Respect for People."

TPS must be mutually beneficial and do no harm to stakeholders. Unfortunately, the same cannot be said of Lean.

The important relationships, shown in the image below, remain largely unknown in Lean, but not in TPS.

Homework Assignment

Continuous Improvement   Respect for People

Identify Relationships Between CI Tools/Methods and RP Principle For Each Category of Stakeholder

If you can do this, then you begin to understand TPS/Lean management

fill in three or more items per cell	Customers	Employees	Suppliers	Investors	Community
Takt Time					
Standardized Work					
Root Cause Anal.					
Heijunka					
Jidoka (automonation)					
Just-in-Time					
Set-Up Reduction					
Kanban					
Mistake-Proofing					
Visual Controls					
Boss's Behaviors					

Used in Prof. Emiliani's graduate Lean leadership course and training programs since ~2004

As Womack and Jones are the producers of Lean and its most visible and enduring proponents, I believe they owe the Lean community answers to these questions:

- Why did 'Respect for People' emerge only recently as a feature of Lean management?
- Why didn't you recognize it sooner?

Questions to consider:

- Would the spread of Lean and its impact on employees, suppliers, and other stakeholders have been more favorable if "Respect for People" had been recognized and presented explicitly at the start, in 1988? Meaning, less damaging to employees (layoffs) and suppliers (price squeeze), and more favorable to investors (higher returns) and communities (continued presence and growth).
- If Lean excluded "Respect for People" at the start and for 20 years thereafter, how could it be characterized as a generic term synonymous with TPS?
- What is Lean if there is no "Respect for People?"
- Is Lean a new management system if it results in the same or similar outcomes as the conventional management practice it is seeking to replace?

Lean = TPS - Umami

Let us again review Professor Monden's 1983 interpretation of TPS [5]:

"...although cost-reduction is the system's most important goal, it must achieve three other sub-goals in order to achieve its primary objective. They include:

1. Quantity control, which enables the system to adapt to daily and monthly fluctuations in demand in terms of quantities and variety;

2. Quality assurance, which assures that each process will supply only good units to subsequent processes;

3. Respect-for-humanity, which must be cultivated while the system utilizes the human resources to obtain its cost objectives.

It should be emphasized here that these three goals cannot exist independently or be achieved independently without influencing each other or the primary goal of cost reduction. It is a special feature of the Toyota production system that the primary goal cannot be achieved without realization of the subgoals and vice versa. All goals are outputs of the same system; with productivity as the ultimate purpose and guiding concept, the Toyota production system strives to realize each of the goals for which it has been designed."

This interpretation is consistent with what I learned from Shingijutsu kaizen consultants more than twenty years ago. It is consistent with the team member handbook that Toyota created in 1984 for its NUMMI joint venture with General Motors [8], and also consistent with Taiichi Ohno's books [9, 10].

As you know, Krafcik's 1988 paper, "Triumph of the Lean Production System" [6] and the influential 1990 book, *The Machine that Changed the World: The Story of Lean Production* [3] by Womack, Jones, and Roos, presented "lean production" as a generic term synonymous with TPS. However, if company A were to practice Lean and company B were to practice TPS, all other things being equal, would the outcomes be the same?

In their influential 1996 book *Lean Thinking: Banish Waste and Create Wealth in Your Corporation* [4], Womack and Jones used the term "lean thinking" to describe what they had learned in their research about the people who were creating Lean (i.e. TPS) organizations. They defined "lean thinking" as consisting of the following five principles that guided people's actions (pp. 10 and 16-26):

1. Specify Value
2. Identify the Value Stream
3. Flow
4. Pull
5. Perfection

Taiichi Ohno and his people did not think this way. The Lean thinking construct is inconsistent with the mindset, thinking, goals, objectives, methods, and outcomes that led to the creation and evolution of TPS.

Lean has proven to be less effective than TPS because it missed many critically important elements. While today some additional elements of TPS are now better recognized, they remain less important in Lean. These include:

- Kaizen
- Respect for people
- Management-employee relations
- Mutual trust and teamwork
- Stable employment

- Human energy, enthusiasm, and passion for improvement
- Evolution in mindset and methods
- Infinite possibilities for improvement
- Hunger for survival

Together, these elements are "the umami of TPS," where *umai* (うまい) means "delicious" and *mi* (味) means "taste." Umami is the fifth taste, savory. Without these elements of TPS, Lean can taste sweet to management and investors, but salty, sour, or bitter to workers who have been harmed by Lean. Therefore,

$$Lean = TPS - Umami.$$

Without umami, Lean cannot produce the business results and people development outcomes that TPS can produce. Said another way, the most successful "Lean" organizations include the umami [1]. Their management practice is closer to TPS than it is to Lean.

Questions to consider:

- Benchmarking a company's methods (through books or first-hand visits) and bringing them back to one's own company typically results in poor outcomes because the context and many other supporting factors are missing. Can Lean be characterized as the product of benchmarking Toyota's methods to account for the differences?
- Toyota Thinking ≠ Lean Thinking. What are the differences between Toyota thinking and Lean thinking?
- How does the association between "wealth creation" and "Lean thinking" change managers' understanding of the purpose and goals of TPS?

- The focus of *The Machine that Changed the World* was a new way of making things. The focus of *Lean Thinking* was wealth creation. Why the change in focus from making things, in which there are vast things for managers to learn, to wealth creation, where there is almost nothing for managers to learn (see Chapter 3, "How Economics Subverts Lean")?

A Moving Target

What is "lean thinking?" Over the last two decades there have been four different definitions. Two definitions in the first ten or eleven years, and two more definitions in the last few years.

In the book *Lean Thinking* [4], Womack and Jones used the term "lean thinking" to describe what they had learned in their research about the people who were creating Lean organizations. They defined "lean thinking" as consisting of the following five principles that guided people's actions (pp. 10 and 16-26):

1. Specify Value
2. Identify the Value Stream
3. Flow
4. Pull
5. Perfection

This initial definition is clearly technocratic. Its focus are the processes used to create value. Womack and Jones also characterized it as a "thinking process" used by the managers and workers who create value.

Then, according the *Lean Lexicon* [11], Womack and Jones "simplified the five steps" in 2006 to [12]:

• Purpose
• Process
• People

This second definition of "lean thinking" is clearly less technocratic. Its focus is broader than the processes used to create value and includes the purpose for an organization's existence and the people (managers and workers) who are involved in value-creating processes.

In a 2014 article titled "What Lean Really Is" [13], Daniel T. Jones offers a third definition (links added to the quote are mine):

> "Lean thinking and practice are generic versions of the Toyota Production System (TPS) and the Toyota Way management system."

This third definition is substantially different from the first and second definitions.

A month later, in an article in *Fast Company* magazine, "10 Signs You Respect Me as an Employee" [14], authors Michael Ballé and Daniel Jones define "lean thinking" in a new way that is different from the earlier definition:

> "Toyota grounded its management on learning and, over the years, developed a continuous on-the-job learning method based on two pillars: continuous improvement–continuously challenging oneself and learning by continuous small steps–and respect–making our best efforts to understand the obstacles each person encounters, supporting their development and making the best possible use of their abilities. We refer to this as 'lean thinking.'"

This fourth definition parallels "The Toyota Way 2001" document [2] which "clarifies the values and business methods that all employees should embrace in order to carry out the Guiding Principles at Toyota throughout the company's global activities." The pillars of the Toyota Way are "Continuous Improvement" and "Respect for People." Importantly, "people" includes not just employees, but customers, shareholders, business partners, and communities.

While people have always been part of these four definitions, you can see that people – employees – take on greater prominence over time, eventually carrying equal weight to the technical steps used to create value. What do these changes in definitions over a period of 18 years tell us?

Questions to consider:

- Did the definitions change as a result of a growing awareness by Womack and Jones that people – employees – are important in Lean; that employees make or break Lean success?
- Do the changing definitions reflect learning or an evolution in thinking that resulted from asking questions, observation, and personal practice? If so, why did it take seven years since the second definition was established or 13 years since "The Toyota Way 2001" was published to see that?
- Do the changing definitions mean that Toyota's management system was poorly understood despite years of close study? And, that "Respect for People" is now recognized as critically important for managers to understand and practice?
- Was the importance of employees understood early-on by Womack and Jones but ignored in preference to satisfying marketplace demand for process improvement (Lean) tools?
- Did the definition change over time to suit one's own business, reputational, or other purpose?

Lean Thinking

The 20th anniversary of the book *Lean Thinking* was marked by two interviews of James P. Womack and Daniel T. Jones. The first was published on the Planet Lean web site on 21 September 2016 [15]. The second was published on the Lean Enterprise Institute web site on 28 and 29 September 2016 [16, 17].

What follows are critiques of selected passages from both interviews, beginning with the 21 September 2016 interview [15]:

> Jim Womack: Our aim was to give people a license to try something new. That's why we structured the book the way we did, in three parts: a simple explanation of what lean is (the five principles)...

Comment: The 5 principles of Lean (Thinking) are a different expression of principles than either TPS or The Toyota Way, thus making Lean significantly different than the Toyota Production System (TPS) and The Toyota Way.

> Dan Jones: I believe that the book succeeded in particular because it spoke to people who were struggling with the challenges brought forward by globalization (like Chinese competition, for example) and with making things better at work to engage a new generation of employees with different expectations about involvement.

Comment: The subtitle of *Lean Thinking* is *Banish Waste and Create Wealth in Your Corporation*. Wealth creation – increasing the stock price – is what resonated with managers in the mid- to late-1990s and thereafter. Globalization led to rapid outsourcing and offshoring to obtain low wages, and widespread layoffs, not the detailed and painstaking work of improving the company's internal processes and developing human capabilities. Managers did not care about what the (then) new generation of employees wanted.

> Dan Jones: At first, people plowed through the tools and, for a long time, they believed that the toolbox was all there was to lean… But I think this was a necessary step to establish the movement and later come to the realization that it is up to management to make lean a success. Now we have gone further, talking about lean as a strategy and a learning process for leaders. We are on the cusp of answering a lot of questions, and we couldn't have done it without this movement, or without its mistakes.

Comment: The problem is the time. These important realizations should have come much sooner to Womack and Jones and their respective organizations, LEI and LEA. The transition from Lean production to Lean management and Lean leadership was too slow. Lean as a strategy is a "slow burn" for stable long-term growth and survival, which is unappealing to leaders who seek fast results. If Lean is now a learning process for senior leaders, one needs to step back and recognize the reality of what that means. Few leaders think they have much new to learn. Womack and Jones surely know this as well.

> Jim Womack: We didn't give people any advice on how to sustain either. For example, there is no discussion at all about creating the basic stability that is the necessary foundation for sustainable kaizen. Dan and I had never been managers and assumed that managers in most organizations would have the energy and ability to sustain results. It turned out they couldn't, and that the management systems of most companies were designed to do re-work on top of chaos, not to sustain kaizen gains. We didn't give any advice on this problem because we weren't aware of it.

Comment: Sustainability is a myth. Leaders can never sustain results (in anything) because things change every day, managers come and go, and organizations are merged or sold. One can never reach a state where Lean resides within the company's DNA. Lean resides in people. Non-Lean thinking is like gravity, constantly pulling people back down. "Three steps forward, one step back" has long been the reality. It is only through daily hard work that Lean moves forward over time. Think of it like a musician's practice. Capabilities decline if one does not practice, and practice, itself, is difficult to sustain long-term.

> Dan Jones: As writers rather than managers, Jim and I could only write what we saw other managers do during our research. Indeed, we assumed people would want to figure lean out by themselves; instead, we discovered they wanted us to tell them what to do.

Comment: The modern history of management (ca. 1880 forward) is littered with examples of managers wanting other people to tell them what to do. And if you succeed in doing that, managers often ignore it. Most managers focus their attention on figuring out the things that are of immediate interest – the metric, the competitive threat, the internal politics, etc. Lean is not well suited for people whose interest in thinking is limited or who are unwilling to abandon their preconceptions.

> Dan Jones: Absolutely. Lean is a people-centric solution, not a people-free solution. Taylorism was about building a system, designed by experts, which any fool could operate, while lean is a management system centered on people and growing out of the gemba.

Comment: This is a common mischaracterization of Frederick Winslow Taylor's work, and also fails to recognize how Taylor's work evolved in his time and thereafter, and its role (as well as Frank and Lillian Gilbreth's work) in laying the foundation for TPS and The Toyota Way. It turns out any fool could *not* operate Scientific Management correctly. That was managers' fault, not Taylor's fault.

> Jim Womack: We had an excellent balance in our way of working, and a wonderful relationship. Dan is a born optimist and a big-picture guy, while I am a born pessimist and obsess over details.

Comment: Womack obsesses over details pertaining to writing the book. Yet, where is the obsession over details of Lean in practice? There has never been much obsession over Fake Lean, Lean failures (see Chapter 3 – "Lean Transformation Process Failure"), the harm done to employees by Lean (e.g. layoffs, caused by managers' misunderstandings), etc. Womack has been a highly visible and outspoken cheerleader for Lean despite obvious problems which seem to have gone unnoticed for many years, and for which the details are apparently unimportant.

> Jim Womack: Our approach was to never be too prescriptive. As exasperating as this was to our orthodox Toyota friends, we have always believed that experimentation and an open mind to try new things are more important than having read the Scriptures. Instead we've said, "Let's go to the gemba, collect some data and let the evidence speak". And that's what the examples in *Lean Thinking* did.

Comment: Womack and Jones could not be too prescriptive even if they wanted to because they lack first-hand experience with TPS, generally, and kaizen in particular. Nevertheless, experimentation and going to the genba come directly from TPS (and Scientific Management before that), not from Lean.

Jim Womack: The Shingijutsu guys were very interesting for a number of reasons. To begin with, they had worked directly with Taiichi Ohno. Secondly, they had done brownfield transformations of Toyota suppliers in Toyota's mad rush to bring its supply base up to its lean standard after sales took off with the Corolla in 1966. So they had both the lean knowledge and a tested transformation method! The latter came in the form of the magical five-day *kaizen*. They would take an area of a factory or office and transform it within a week by introducing cells and one-piece flow (so it was *kaikaku* more than it was kaizen). It was a brilliant technique, but it was incomplete – you have to kaizen and kaikaku both the value stream and the management at the same time if you are going to succeed, but there was no method for the latter... The Shingijutsu team achieved impressive if often unsustainable results every time, which made them very popular consultants.

Comment: Shingijutsu kaizen consultants [18] had TPS knowledge. They do not know anything about Lean (but they have heard of it). Kaikaku is the one-time gain going from batch-and-queue to flow (or flow limited by supermarkets). The ongoing, day-to-day kaizen after Shingijutsu departs is the responsibility of management, which Shingijutsu makes clear, but which management usually fails at. This is not Shingijutsu's fault. No single method exists to get senior managers to do what they do not want to do. Shingijutsu teaches people Toyota-style kaizen – the heart, the mind, and the method (with unique Shingijutsu elements). It is complete if one accepts it. As with any consultant, it is not Shingijutsu's responsibility to sustain their client's results. Management often fails in its responsibility, as Womack and Jones know first-hand in their consulting work with executives from Delphi, Tesco, and many others. To think otherwise reveals a large perceptual gap. The simple facts are that the understanding, know-how, and capabilities of Shingijutsu consultants far exceeds that of Womack and Jones.

Dan Jones: Lean is all about practice and experiments, which we wrote about and interpreted. I think that the fact that academia is only now picking up on *Lean Thinking* says a lot.

Comment: Lean is indeed an interpretation of TPS, and, nearly 20 years later, of The Toyota Way. Academics are not the only ones behind the times.

Jim   Womack: Sadly,   academia   was   much   more comfortable with theory and with studies using large numbers of examples for statistical analysis. This means there is always a perceptual gap and a time lag with reality in their work. The view from the rearview mirror.

Comment: True as a generality, but not all academics suffer from perceptual gaps and time lags with reality (see the Appendix).

Dan Jones: There is much more to lean than we originally thought and, so long as we keep digging and learning, we can rest assured that the movement will keep growing.

Comment: If Lean is understood to be the generic term for TPS and The Toyota Way, then there is indeed much to learn, especially through direct experience. If Lean is something different than TPS and The Toyota Way, then there is far less to learn.

• • • • •

Critique of selected passages from the second interview on 28 and 29 September 2016 [16, 17]:

> Jim: ...organizations struggle to make good margins, customers report declining confidence in the ability of providers to solve their problems, and employees report low engagement and a lack of satisfaction in their work... Lean thinking was and is the best-known way to sustainably improve this situation.

Comment: There is a large body of empirical evidence that, when it comes to improvement via Lean, sustainability is elusive. It is akin to knowing how to play a music instrument; a reduction in practice results in a decline in capabilities. Likewise, a decline in curiosity to learn more about the instrument and music results in stagnant or declining capabilities. It is better to not seek or think in terms of sustainability. Instead, think as sensei Nagamatsu-san does [18]: "We are always at our worst. You may think you are a good company today, but make no mistake you are not. You may become better tomorrow, but still you are toward the back. At any moment, somewhere in this world there is someone doing the same work better. There is no end. You must continually seek to improve."

> Dan Jones: Perhaps the biggest lesson is that there is much more to lean than they [top management] (and we) thought...

Comment: A perplexing comment. Womack and Jones' association with Toyota leaders should have quickly taught them the infinite nature of kaizen. This realization was apparently late in coming and therefore inadequately conveyed to top managers interested in Lean.

Dan Jones: The unique power of these practices is that they can't be dismissed as not working – they are alive and working in our continuing reference model Toyota.

Comment: But often, the practices don't work or don't work correctly in Lean. More importantly, Lean can be easily dismissed by top managers because they have many quicker and easier ways to "improve" the business, as shown below.

What Lean Competes Against

CEO PLAYBOOK FOR IMPROVING BUSINESS RESULTS	DEGREE OF DIFFICULTY (10 = highest)	TIME TO EXECUTE (years)
Robots / Automation / AI	2	1-2
Layoffs	1	1
Hire New Managers	1	<<1
Close Facilities	1	<1
Stock Buy-Backs	1	1-3
Acquisition	2	1
Merger	2	1
Divest / Spin Off Assets	1	1
Change Incentive Compensation	1	<1
Develop New Products	2	1-2
Develop New Markets	3	1-5
Discontinue Products / Services	1	<<1
Reduce / Increase Debt	1	<1
Change Accounting Method	2	<1-2
Reduce Taxes / Move Offshore	2	1
Consolidate Operations	2	1-2
New Equipment / Technology	1	1-3
Outsource (common method)	2	1-2
Squeeze Suppliers on Price	1	<<1
Price Cuts / Increases	1	<<1
Budget Cuts	1	<1
Lobby Gov't for Cuts in Taxes & Regs	2	1-3

Lean may have been an attempt to make TPS more user-friendly and thus diminish the degree of difficulty between it and other methods shown above. But, this has been unsuccessful so far. In addition, leaders do not see Lean as strategic, but rather as a tactical way for workers to improve processes.

Jim Womack: But the creation of true lean enterprises combining lean techniques with lean management has hardly been achieved anywhere. We are still at the beginning of the lean transformation!

Comment: Thirty-five years after Frederick Winslow Taylor's death, his associate, Harlow Person, said [19]: "In the course of his [1912] testimony before the House committee [to Investigate the Taylor and Other Systems of Shop Management], Taylor was asked how many concerns [companies] used his system in its entirety. His reply was: 'In its entirety – none; not one.' Then, in response to another question he went on to say that a great many used it substantially, to a greater or less degree. Were Mr. Taylor alive to respond to the same question in 1947 – thirty-five years later – his reply would have to be essentially the same." It seems we are re-living history.

Jim Womack: I've said since *Lean Thinking* was launched with the thought that its most important contribution would be to give managers the courage to try their own experiments.

Comment: Business history informs us that few managers are courageous in the ways necessary for progressive management to thrive.

Jim Womack: The two points we did make [in the book] – and that many lean adopters in senior management have ignored – are 1) that lean is not about cost-cutting but about providing more value by means of a better value-creating process and 2) that the work experience will improve when everyone can see the whole value stream and the consequences of their own efforts and get feedback continuously and instantly on how to improve the results while making work easier.

Comment: The subtitle of the book, *Banish Waste and Create Wealth in Your Corporation*, did not signal these two points to top managers. In fact, it signaled Lean as a means to increase stock price by improving processes, with the added financial gain of laying off employees.

Dan Jones: ... "people-centric" solutions are cheaper to start, cheaper to maintain, more exactly focused on the varied needs of users and waste far less resources, while at the same time they can easily adapt to changing circumstances. Lean provides an alternative voice to the relentless march of those seeking "people-free" solutions.

Comment: We must consider the possibility that Lean will be made irrelevant or eclipsed by the relentless (and increasingly rapid) advancement of technology. As the great Frank George Woollard [20] said long ago, "We must always remember that men were not made for machines, but that machines were made for man... the motto must be... 'Machines in the Service of Man'."

Dan Jones: First, lean has to be seen as strategic, and therefore top management has to be convinced about the business case for lean. In our enthusiasm to carry out proof of concept experiments to show how lean works we failed to give this sufficient attention.

Comment: The history of progressive management is littered with those who have attempted to convince top managers that progressive management is strategic. Many before Womack and Jones have tried and failed.

Jim Womack: I hope it is simply that the life of lean is experiments, not dogma.

Comment: Dogma is built into Lean (and TPS), and therefore inescapable. And so are its consequences, one of which is a failure to learn from others.

Jim Womack: The problem is with "thinking." That's passive rather than active and we brought up this point with our editor as we were preparing the book for launch. "How about 'lean transformation' or something that conveys the necessity of learning by trying experiments?" To which the editor – looking at sales of the book rather than the effect of the book on managers – said, "People love to think, which has no risk. But they hate to act, which is dangerous. So let's stick with lean thinking. That title will sell." And at that time publishing contracts always stated "the publisher retains the right to title the work." So...we got Lean Thinking.

Comment: Interesting insights into the motivation of publishers versus the motivation of authors. The subtitle, *Banish Waste and Create Wealth in Your Corporation*, was not mentioned as a problem, which it was, because it cued top managers to see Lean as a way to increase the stock price – typically at employees' expense.

Dan Jones: The more I think about it the more I think that Lean Thinking was the right title for the book, although I would now add "and Practice." Practice in both senses of the word; practice as in the many hours learning to play the violin (daily Kaizen) and practice as the way your approach any problem in life.

Comment: Learning how to play music is an excellent analogy [21]. Kaizen is indeed the key. The question is, why has kaizen has not been of greater prominence in the advancement of Lean? The emphasis has been on value stream maps, A3 reports, genba walks, and so on. The focus should be on kaizen and flow.

Dan Jones: At its heart, lean is a cognitive revolution and not an organizational one. Lean thinking cannot be learnt from abstract thinking alone, but only through repeated, structured practice with "ah-ha" insights as to why common notions are wrong – in other words, "by acting our way to a new way of thinking." This applies as much to top managers as it does to front-line teams, "you learn by helping others to learn."

Comment: Lean is merely the current name for a version of progressive management modeled after TPS, which was pioneered by Frederick Winslow Taylor in the late 1800s. In his book, *The Principles of Scientific Management*, Taylor said [22]: "…the really great problem involved in a change from the management of 'initiative and incentive' [conventional management] to scientific management consists in a complete revolution in the mental attitude and the habits of all those engaged in the management, as well as of the workmen." It has therefore long been recognized that progressive management requires a mental or cognitive revolution. Note that Taylor said this applies to workers as well as managers. Both must experience a mental revolution. Hands-on practice by both managers and workers is necessary but not sufficient, as there are multiple dimensions to the mental revolution beyond the work itself. One dimension is economics, and it is perhaps the most powerful dimension in its ability to thwart the mental revolution.

Questions to consider:

- Throughout the history of progressive management, its proponents have struggled to gain the attention of senior managers and broaden its appeal. After exhausting numerous approaches, the final characterization of progressive management presented to business leaders is as a strategy. This too has proven unsuccessful. Will the outcome for Lean be any different? Why or why not?
- Is there a demand among senior managers for a "complete revolution in the mental attitude and the habits?" Why or why not?
- Hands-on practice is essential for learning TPS (and Lean). Is that something senior managers want to do?
- Can Lean management prosper in organizations if leaders think they have little to learn? What can be done about that?
- Do business leaders care more for "people-centric solutions" or technology-centric solutions? What does history tell us?
- After 30 years, why has Lean remained a niche management practice?

3

Ignoring the Big Problems

Learning to Not See

How does Lean look to outside observers? Many critics see Lean as flim-flam or cult-like because stories about Lean success outnumber stories about Lean failure by a huge margin [1-3]. How is it that success can come so easily, when success is hard to come by in far simpler endeavors? Critics also witness homage paid to Lean's patriarchs at conferences, and on social media where Lean people heartily congratulate each other on insignificant accomplishments.

The reality is this: Decades after Lean came into being, most organizations still practice Fake Lean (defined as "Continuous Improvement" only, no "Respect for People") or have been unsuccessful. The collective effort has been a failure by any measure, including the seemingly favorable measure that "every major corporation has got a Lean program" [4]. There remains a large gap between intended outcomes and actual outcomes that must be closed. While the cause of the gap is many and varied, the great difference between TPS and Lean has surely played an important role.

It seems unethical and misleading to cheerlead Lean successes and ignore or downplay Lean failures. It is easy to understand why people do this – to maintain popular interest in Lean and to satisfy self-interest – but that weakens, rather than strengthens, credibility. Misleading people does not respect people. It does not clearly inform them of the many and varied significant personal and organizational challenges they must undertake. Business leaders are driven to make uninformed decision in the hope that they will change how they lead and make other necessary adjustments once they finally realize the worthwhile journey they are on. Unfortunately, the vast majority of leaders never do.

Knowledge is advanced by critical thinking followed by problem-solving using the Scientific Method. The Lean community knows this well, but is inconsistent; it knows what to do but often does not actually do it in relation to its own problems. Instead, abnormal conditions are ignored and positive feedback welcomed despite it obscuring reality.

The Lean community must return to the basics that it has long advocated: Look at the facts, see reality as it actually is, and make improvements. It must reflect, talk forthrightly about abnormalities, and begin by asking "Why?"

The conversations, and subsequent actions, should be around important questions such as these:

- Why is there inconsistent use of the Scientific Method when it comes to promoting or advancing Lean?
- Why weren't the people who said TPS was not a bunch of tools listened to (e.g. Ohno)?
- Why did organizations replace kaizen with tools such as value stream maps, A3 reports, gemba walks, etc?
- Why did it take so long to recognize Lean as a management system?
- Why did it take so long to realize the nature and importance of Lean leadership?
- Why is it that improved behaviors are still seen as the only countermeasure for poor leadership?
- Why were Lean producers and users quiet when people were laid off as a result of Lean (esp. 1990-2014)?
- Why was it not understood that Lean must do no harm?
- Why do most Lean transformations fail?
- Why don't we formally analyze Lean transformation failures and learn from them?
- Why isn't Lean management widely taught in business schools?

Lean conferences should address these and other important questions in the same manner that scientific conferences address important questions, instead of simply showcasing success stories. These questions could be conference tracks with speakers presenting their data and analyses, followed by discussion and critiques by attendees. The will result in many new practical ideas for improvement.

Scientific inquiry has a better chance of transforming Lean from a niche management practice into a more common management practice that results in mutually beneficial outcomes for all stakeholders. It is an opportunity to learn, improve, and respect humanity.

Questions to consider:

- The many Lean success stories are not lies, but they are not the whole story either. Why not present the whole story [5], so that people can learn more and make informed judgments?
- Do success stories, far outnumbering failure stories, undercut the credibility of Lean, as well as the credibility of its originators and users?
- Why doesn't the Lean community take a scientific approach to problem-solving when it comes to Lean's problems?
- Why are success stories the focus of Lean conferences when the purported mindset of Lean people is scientific thinking [6]?
- Can learning, as an outcome, be characterized as "success" when a stakeholder has been harmed by the zero-sum application of Lean (i.e. Fake Lean)?

Lean Transformation Process Failure

Organizations that promote Lean management teach people how to focus on the process, think scientifically, observe, conduct experiments, engage in structured problem-solving, identify root causes, respect people, improve continuously, and, above all, learn. Yet, when to comes to Lean transformations, the focus is Lean success while Lean failures are ignored. Good science looks at all the data, not just the data that one likes. Ignoring Lean failures goes against everything the producers of Lean teach and gives the appearance of having a greater interest in self-promotion than actual Lean success, and more interest in their fate than their customers' fate.

The ubiquity of Fake Lean informs us that there are significant defects in the Lean transformation process that contribute to failure. The steady volume of complaints about Lean by workers over the years should have been an unmistakable signal that a big problem existed and therefore need attending to. But that has not yet happened, despite nearly three decades of clear signals. Shouldn't a scientific approach be taken to this problem as well? What are the Lean transformation process defects? What are their root causes? And what countermeasures can be applied to prevent them from occurring?

As an engineer trained in formal failure analysis methods and having applied it for many years in industry, I have always thought it important to apply that same reasoning and process to business and management failures, including failed Lean transformations. Unfortunately, when such failures occur, most people ignore causes, guess at causes, or simply move on. And they apply ineffective countermeasures based on guesses, such as personnel changes or a re-organization of departments. Senior managers, shareholders, unions, the business press, and other stakeholders don't care about failure analysis. As a result, the learning is lost, and the failure will be repeated sometime in the future and cause harm to employees and other stakeholders.

As the image on the next page shows, there is as much, if not more, to learn from failure than success.

Discussion about Lean management revolves around the worker who is doing value-added work, and how management must support workers. Yet, it is not just management that must support the workers, the producers of Lean must do so as well. It seems irresponsible to promote Lean yet not investigate failures to determine root causes and countermeasures.

Formal engineering-type failure analysis should be applied to Lean transformation to illuminate the precise source of the problems so that corrections can be made to prevent future failures. Without such analysis, no corrections are made and the failures continue unabated, causing much frustration and damage to people and organizations. Worker's persistent complaints about Fake Lean must not be ignored.

Lean transformation process failure is real. Taiichi Ohno recognized the existence of success and failure in relation to TPS:

- "Unless all sources of waste are detected and crushed, success will always be just a dream" [7].

- "We are doomed to failure without a daily destruction of our various preconceptions" [8].

- "... those who decide to implement the Toyota production system must be fully committed. If you try to adopt only the 'good parts', you'll fail" [9].

Root Cause Analysis of Lean Transformation Failure

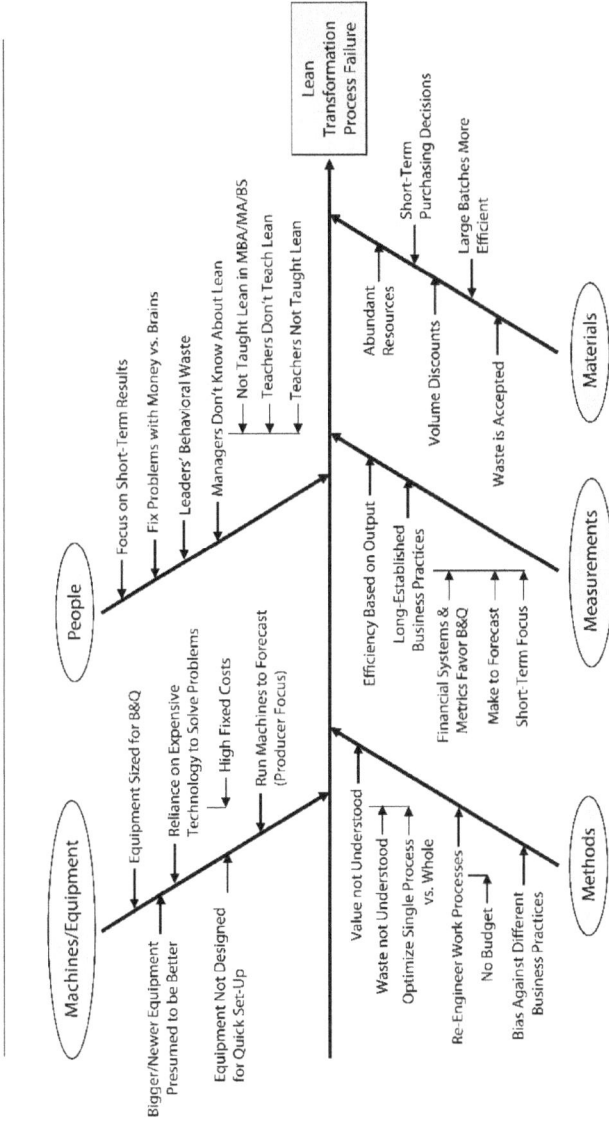

Early (ca. 2001) root cause analysis of Lean transformation process failure used in Prof. Emiliani's (then) new Lean Leadership course.

The basic way of thinking in TPS is that things are a mess and there have lots and lots of problems – very ugly problems whose existence are real and cannot be denied. These problems need to be recognized, understood, and improved. This is not the basic way of thinking in Lean. The basic way of thinking is Lean is that if you are trying, you are learning. And that is good enough.

In Lean, there is a strong focus on problem-solving using the scientific method and its derivatives (PDCA, kaizen, A3s, etc.) to improve *some* processes, but not all processes. As the saying goes, "You can't improve if you don't know about problems." This negative perspective informs TPS and should inform Lean as well.

If Lean transformation process failures are ignored, then there is an accompanying failure to acknowledge problems and an obvious disrespect people created by denying the existence of serious problems that people have experienced – and which may have caused them harm.

The following pages contain an open letter addressed to the Lean Enterprise Institute and the Lean Enterprise Academy posted on Twitter and LinkedIn suggesting that they are remiss in their duties by not focusing on Lean transformation process failures because such failures are ubiquitous and because there is much to learn from them. And, because their customers deserve a better product.

Questions to consider:

- The focus of Lean is using scientific thinking for problem-solving and improvement. Why isn't this carried forward when it comes to Lean failure, either by the producers of Lean or by the organizations that suffer Lean failure?
- In TPS, there is a great effort to remove workers' struggles and simplify work. Why isn't this same way of thinking applied to Lean transformation, where workers and managers clearly struggle?
- Can Lean be considered a successful movement if Lean transformation cannot be achieved on a more widespread basis?
- Can Lean be considered a successful movement if the extent of Lean practice is the use of selected tools?
- Every organization struggles with Lean transformation, and most suffer significant setbacks or failure. Is the credibility of Lean strengthened or weakened by ignoring failures?

An Open Letter to the Lean Enterprise Institute
and the Lean Enterprise Academy

28 February 2016

As the recognized leaders of the Lean movement, I am dismayed by the continuing lack of interest in understanding the root causes of failed Lean transformations. As you know, Fake Lean is far more prevalent than successful Real Lean transformations. While success stories are uplifting and helpful, failed Lean transformations are more valuable. They offer hundreds of opportunities to learn and improve so that workers and other stakeholders are not harmed in the future.

Workers suffer under Fake Lean, which must be recognized and responded to with both sympathy and meaningful action. To not do the most one can to understand the causes of failure and identify countermeasures to help eliminate worker suffering undercuts the credibility of Lean management and diminishes the strength and vitality of the Lean movement, an important cause for which we are all deeply committed.

For nearly 30 years, red andon lights have been turned on in businesses worldwide signaling Lean transformation process problems. Workers are concerned, frustrated, and tired of Fake Lean. Articles critical of Lean mount day-by-day, only to be exceeded by personal stories critical of Lean. Yet, indifference to the plight of workers suggests large gap exists between belief in "Respect for People" and concrete actions. To the extent possible, workers must be protected from Fake Lean.

As leaders of the movement, I believe you are duty-bound to formally analyze Lean failures whenever and wherever it is possible to do so. A good place to begin is with a U.K. grocer and other organizations whose leadership teams you have coached and instructed in Lean management, but where outcomes have faltered. The results of the detailed failure analyses then become a new and important training opportunity for you to help people avoid future failures.

Failed Lean transformations have been my area of study since the mid-1990s, with a particular focus on leadership. So, rather than start from scratch, I hope you have interest in building on this body of work. I offer to you a complete suite of my books and papers on this topic. I also offer to you my A4 failure analysis method template, which has been used successfully for over a decade to formally analyze management failures. I ask for nothing in return.

I am well aware that formal failure analysis might not have a great impact or change things to anyone's full satisfaction. Yet, it is important to try and progress will surely be made, as Lean people are resourceful, creative, and innovative. The benefits of formal failure analysis, if they cannot be secured for the present, will surely be helpful to people in the future.

Sincerely,

Bob Emiliani, Ph.D.
Professor of Lean Management
Connecticut State University
New Britain, Connecticut

• • • • •

Response from LEI: Silence
Response from LEA: Silence

Lean for Capital, Not Labor

The Gilded Age was an era between 1870 and 1900, marked by industrialization, mechanization, economic growth, the rise of large corporations, build-out of railways, urbanization, and immense wealth creation for owners of large businesses. It also included monopolies, worker abuse, child labor, corruption, and other conditions that unsettled the American public and which thereby influenced political elections after the turn of the century.

The Progressive Era (ca. 1900-1930) followed the Gilded Age, and was a response to widespread economic and social injustice of the Gilded Age. Progressive movement leaders sought to restore economic and social fairness through various means, including the management of enterprises both large and small. The leader of this part of the Progressive movement was Frederick Winslow Taylor.

The focus of Taylor's work was not technological innovation or mechanization of production resulting from capital investment in the latest machinery. Rather, it was to improve labor productivity via process improvement using existing machines, tools, and materials. The use of a simple stopwatch to determine the time it actually took to do the work was largely the extent of Taylor's interest in mechanisms. Taylor developed his new management system in specific ways whose intended outcomes were to benefit both labor and management (as well as customers), not benefit management at the expense of labor as had been the case during the Gilded Age.

Scientific Management was not created for the purpose of wealth creation, nor was TPS. It was created to improve work processes and cooperation between management and workers, from which both greater profits for owners and higher wages for workers would be realized, as well as many other benefits.

The Toyota production system has roots in the American progressive era and the ideas of cooperation, process improvement, fairness, and mutual prosperity. TPS is recognized as a progressive management practice because it represents reform, innovation, advancement, and improvement over conventional management. TPS is non-zero-sum through its recognition that "Respect for People" is a requirement for its correct practice and to achieve its goals and objectives.

Conventional management is zero-sum. It is devoid of "Respect for People" because that is seen by managers as interfering with the goal of capital accumulation, typically in the short-term. In TPS, specific methods and tools are used by managers and employees to expose problems, understand problems, and continuously improve processes to satisfy customers and earn profits over the long-term. In conventional management, any method or tool that helps fix the problem *du jour* is used, typically in confusing, unsystematic, bureaucratic, and incomplete ways.

Managers in industry became aware of Lean post-1988, principally though the publication of *"Triumph of the Lean Production System"* [10], followed by the books *The Machine that Changed the World – The Story of Lean Production* [11], and *Lean Thinking: Banish Waste and Create Wealth in Your Corporation* [12]. The timing of these works, each devoid of the "Respect for People" principle, could not have been better if a business leader's objective was to create wealth in zero-sum ways; to enrich owners at the expense of employees. Lean became popular just-in-time to contribute to the creation of the Second Gilded Age.

Scientific Management sought to correct economic and social injustice, not to create it. Yet, most owners who adopted Scientific Management used it to create further economic and social injustice. In 1988, Lean emerged as an improved method of management with no clear objective to correct economic and social injustice. As a result, Lean was used by the leaders of large corporations for the purpose of creating wealth for owners in a time of great wealth accumulation not seen since the Gilded Age.

For employees, the timing for Lean could not have been worse. The zero-sum use of Lean combined with the "maximize shareholder value" mantra of CEOs, outsourcing, and offshoring work to low wage countries meant employees would be the biggest losers and owners the biggest winners. For decades, the producers of Lean were silent with respect to the harm that came to employees as Lean was used by business leaders to help expand corporate wealth creation.

Questions to consider:

- As the Second Gilded Age comes to a close, will Lean be used in a different way, to correct economic and ·social injustice and restore fairness in relationships between employees, suppliers, and communities, while still satisfying investors' interests?
- Can Lean survive if it does not deliver financial and non-financial benefits to workers?
- Will business leaders change their understanding of Lean in the coming years to deliver better outcomes for employees, suppliers, and communities?
- Will employees trust Lean or their leaders to deliver better financial and non-financial outcomes for them?
- Is Lean relevant post-2017 in the sense that we have known it since 1988?
- It is still necessary to distinguish between Lean and TPS, and diminish the former and better understand and practice the latter?
- Is the future of Lean only where it is seen in a positive light, such as Lean Startup, Lean product development, or Lean for the environment and natural resource conservation?

- Should Lean (1988 *et sequentes* 2017) be abandoned, tainted by its use as a zero-sum mechanism for corporate wealth creation, and re-booted as "Lean 2.0" or "Second Generation Lean (2G-Lean)?"

How Economics Subverts Lean

It is a worthwhile endeavor to gain deeper insights into the relationship between classical and neoclassical economics and the prevalence and persistence of Fake Lean (defined as "Continuous Improvement" only, no "Respect for People"). The two are not normally associated with one another. However, the narrow use of Lean by business leaders for the purpose of zero-sum cost-cutting, in the furtherance of profit, requires a closer look.

While economics is not the singular cause of Fake Lean, its presence exists on at least three bones of the fishbone diagram: people, methods, and measures. Economics, therefore, is a very important cause that surely contributes to the observed effect, Fake Lean. Economic thought operates in conjunction with business thought. Lean management operates within the realm of business. Therefore, economics seems to play an important role in informing business leaders about conventional management and dis-informing them about progressive management.

This leads to two interesting questions:

- How and to what extent does classical and neoclassical economics interfere with business leaders' ability to understand and lead buyers' market, demand-driven TPS?
- How and to what extent does classical and neoclassical economics interfere with organizations' efforts to correctly practice buyers' market, demand-driven TPS and thus avoid Fake Lean?

Certain core economic ideas developed centuries ago in England quickly became fixed in the minds of business leaders and remain with us to this day. The most interesting critiques of classical economics were made by those who were closer to it in time than we are now, and closer in time to the days when craft work and providing for the community were dominant features of daily human existence.

Books of particular interest include [13-16]:

- *Unto This Last*, John Ruskin, 1862
- *A History of Political Economy*, John Ingram, 1888
- *The Modern Factory System*, Richard Cook-Taylor, 1891
- *The Theory of Business Enterprise*, Thorstein Veblen, 1904

These are insightful works about the past that inform the present. They offer to us an understanding of more than just the inner workings of conventional business leaders' mindset and decision-making. They identify gaps in relation to how Lean has been understood by leaders and practiced by organizations over the last 30 years, as well as how its predecessor, Scientific Management, was understood and practiced in the late 19th and early 20th century.

The critic's detailed and careful analysis of classical economics, business, and management decision-making were typically grounded in facets of daily living, with reference to the virtuous characteristics of mankind created by God and as informed by religious writings and tradition. They were deeply skeptical of certain aspects of political economy, and questioned claims made as to its standing as a science, likening it instead to astrology, for example. It is noteworthy that pioneers of modern economic thought lacked scientific training and were "regarded with ill-disguised contempt" by actual scientists in part due to their blind allegiance to generalizations of human character.

The critics viewed science as something that helps people labor for that which supports or improves life. Political economy, with its acceptance of zero-sum outcomes, was seen as something that did the opposite and therefore resulted in destruction. The religious overtones of the critiques clearly indicate that such outcomes were new and unwelcome additions to human existence. Thus, ideas central to classical economics were seen as lacking in the moral dimensions integral to human ideals and human existence as bestowed by God. Key concepts of political economics that these authors found to be very troubling include:

Economic man: This fictitious abstraction of mankind removes all other human variables to simplify investigation and analysis of economic phenomena. However, as God did not create such a man, none can actually exist, thereby negating economics both as a science and as a true guide for business owners.

Self-interest: The pursuit of self-interest and personal (material) gain were seen as secondary motives to one's work. The prime motive for one's work is service, self-sacrifice, to fellow human beings and the community – this is the sole characteristic that constitutes a "noble" or "great profession." Self-sacrifice must be embedded in business, not "economic man," whose quest for gain is happily pursued in zero-sum fashion. "Self-interest" precludes business from consideration as one of the "great professions."

Profit-seeking: This was seen as a base motive, one that grossly conflicted with the virtue of self-sacrifice. "Money-gain" was not viewed as true gain. The number of happy human beings was seen as the measure of richness. Profit-seeking brought wealth to owners and poverty to workers, and made it difficult for workers to feel affiliated with an organization knowing that owners may cast them aside at any moment and thereby fracturing human relations.

Laissez-faire: The concept of "let it go," self-regulation, was seen by critics as "the devil's philosophy," an excuse for leaders to avoid their responsibilities to lead, to avoid work, and to avoid providing for the community to sustain life. Relatedly, there was strong moral disagreement with the idea that wealth unjustly derived is economically equivalent to wealth justly derived, the latter resulting in inequalities in wealth that disadvantaged workers and community interests.

Natural rights: Human being's intrinsic or natural rights to life, liberty, and property, where ownership is given by one's own work or by trade or by inheritance. Particularly, freedom by an owner to do as he wishes with his property, the business, and all material and human resources contained within it – to the detriment of the community.

In different ways and to varying degrees, these classical economic concepts were seen anti-human, un-human, or working against human interests given by God; e.g. of cooperation (teamwork), community, work, livelihood, and life. Respect and service, self-sacrifice (unselfishness), are intertwined. Remove self-sacrifice, and one removes respect. Thus, the foundation is laid for trickery and deceit in pursuit of one's own interests, which leads straight to destruction. According to Cooke-Taylor, "The motive of self-interest leads men to wrong-doing more often than to right-doing, and should therefore be replaced by the motive of public interest."

The critics decried the acceptance of these five economic ideas with no critical thought, particularly those that exempted humanity from money-making. They viewed elements of classical economics as deeply disrespectful of people. It corrupts and compromises the virtuous gifts that God gave to humans, and reduces God's influence and lowers His rank. People were seen as the true source of wealth, and service as the true purpose of one's work.

Yet, the economic concepts cited above were quickly adopted by businessmen, most likely because they confirmed their biases. Unable to objectively judge the value of the human or his work, businessmen were easily able to objectively judge all matters in relation to "pecuniary interests." These economic ideas soon became a "habit of mind" immune to criticism or re-consideration. They became entrenched for nearly two centuries and could not be appealed no matter how cogent the argument was.

Work, enmeshed with economics, must develop one's humanity, not remove it. The combination of classical economic concepts, profit-seeking, and complex machinery were seen as a detriment to the further development of workers' humanity, impairing their ability to absorb the world around them and bring forth their imagination and creativity into their work, and was, therefore, soul-destroying.

Borrowing from Veblen, one can sum up by saying:

"[Economics], their master, is no respecter of persons
and knows neither morality nor dignity nor
prescriptive rights, divine or human."

So how does this relate to Lean management? The common thread that runs through the five classical economic concepts is disrespect for people. They give explicit permission to owners and managers to disrespect people in the furtherance of business ends. They either greatly discount or completely disregard "Respect for People," both in its casual definition and especially its many meanings within the context of progressive management (i.e. TPS).

Classical economics, therefore, clearly introduces a defect into business leaders' thinking in relation to Lean management, disrespect for people, which is deeply consequential in terms of its human impact and ability to achieve flow. Discarding the "Respect for People" principle allows leaders to avoid work in the same way that *laissez-faire* was seen as an excuse for leaders to avoid work.

Progressive management is meant to achieve many things. Among them is the restoration of economic and social fairness to employees, not the opposite as these ideas in classical economics compel business leaders to do. If business owners' thinking is suffused with these five key economic concepts, then it is logical to conclude that "Respect for People" is of little or no interest. This renders itself as a rigid structural problem in the advancement of both TPS and its derivative, Lean management.

The practical consequence is that people are treated as costs that owners can dispose of as dictated by necessity or whim, to assure continuity of profit. Because this is the prevailing "habit of mind" among business leaders, the prevailing outcome will be Fake Lean. This confirms what has long been evident in actual practice. Fake Lean abounds while Real Lean and TPS flounder.

Instead of embracing demand-driven buyers' markets, classical economics forces business leaders to remain committed to supply-driven sellers' markets. In most cases, the actual markets that organizations face are buyers' markets, yet the management thinking and practice is rooted in 100-year old sellers' markets. This mismatch between market and management system obviously harms the economic interests of the firm as well as its stakeholders.

Is there a remedy? If so, what could it be? A way forward lies in re-thinking how business leaders are introduced to and trained in progressive management. There are likely other ways forward that will need to be used in combination, but let me put this one forward for now: Kaizen.

One of the things we learn from participating in kaizen is that we have much to unlearn about our knowledge of processes and people. As we dive deeper into Lean management, we discover many more things to unlearn and many completely new things to learn. Often, we learn things later that we wished we had learned closer to the beginning of our Lean experience, as this would have helped us move forward faster. One of the most profound learnings is how to process material and information such that it is highly responsive to customer demand in buyers' markets.

For many years, and to this day, Lean leadership training begins with process improvement tools, leadership behaviors, or both. These should no longer come first; they should come later – perhaps much later. Lean leadership training must begin with leaders' beliefs, and in this context, their beliefs about economics. If a leader's understanding of economics is such that it excludes the "Respect for People" principle, and forces them remain committed to the structure and processes characteristic of supply-driven sellers' markets, then it is pointless to train them in process improvement tools or how to improve their behaviors.

For business leaders, Lean training must have a different starting point. As one would fight fire with fire, one must fight pecuniary interests with pecuniary interests. Specifically, the ideas embedded in classical economics that create a "habit of mind" that discounts humanity and results in Fake Lean – as well as the inability to efficiently serve the buyers' markets that the firm actually faces.

Business leaders must be shown how certain ideas in classical economics conflict with both of the bedrock principles of Toyota management, "Continuous Improvement" and "Respect for People," as the two are deeply interwoven and necessary for efficiently serving buyers' markets. The economic mindset and management method must change in order to experience the wide-ranging benefits of TPS over the long-term. Kaizen is the key.

It is clear that the focus and methods of training business leaders – process improvement tools and new behaviors – cannot remain the same. While the faulty economic concepts that business leaders learned about in college or graduate school will continue to be taught, the learning can be undone. Almost everything about TPS is learned on-the-job, and so it must be when it comes to the nexus of economics, markets, and TPS.

Questions to consider:

- Classical and neoclassical economics subverts TPS, a progressive management systems designed to respond to demand-driven buyers' markets. Why do business leaders see as their imperative the need to preserve the superiority of capital over consumer? Why not accept consumer over capital? Is that were to happen, would the actual overall effect on capital be favorable or unfavorable?

- Capitalist experimentation (TPS created by industrial engineers through trial-and-error) achieved what economists (social scientists) have been unable to do through reasoning, mathematical equations, or models, which is to create a practical approach to customer-first as a proxy for capital-first in the work of production. Why did the capitalist experiment (TPS) result in better outcomes for capital and workers compared to what economists have been able to achieve since the late 18th century?

- Executives who adopt TPS or Real Lean confront the need to change economics or change Lean. Invariably they prefer change Lean and adopt Fake Lean. Why are the vast majority of executives unwilling to change their understanding of economics? Why have only a small minority of executives been willing to transition to the economic (as well as the social and political constructs) that TPS (or Real Lean) demands?

- Generation after generation of business leaders are schooled in classical and neoclassical economics, which is inconsistent with TPS. Besides kaizen, what else can be done to align leaders understanding of economics with TPS?

- The common thread that runs through the five economic concepts is disrespect for people. A pillar of the Toyota Way is "Respect for People." In what other ways can this massive dichotomy be reconciled?

- The five economic concepts have become a "habit of mind" largely immune to criticism or re-consideration by economists and business leaders. Why?

- How do you reconcile the five economic concepts with the requirements that TPS must do no harm to stakeholders?

- If the prime motive for one's work is service, self-sacrifice, to fellow human beings and the community, what should the producers of Lean do differently in the future?

4

Failure to Improve

Selective Adoration

Every day, thousands of people confuse Lean management with "Taylorism," properly known as Scientific Management. The negative association brings out the Lean movement leaders and others who work hard to create a great separation between Lean and Taylor. This is an ill-informed and inappropriate response. It is also an irresponsible response because it misleads people. The leaders of the Lean movement, in particular, should not mislead people through their own prejudice and ignorance. And those who speak loudest about "Respect for People" are quick to shower Frederick Winslow Taylor with disrespect and other forms of disdain and mistreatment.

Taylorism has been a heavy anchor around Lean's neck for more than 30 years, and it will continue to be unless a wiser strategy is undertaken in response to confusion between Scientific Management and Lean management. Rather than trying to paint Frederick Winslow Taylor as a villain, which he was not, the smarter and more accurate action is to respect Taylor and recognize him for his accomplishments and how his work, and that of his colleagues, were necessary first steps in the evolution of progressive management that helped pave the way for Toyota's management system decades later. Toyota made use of Taylor's time studies, Frank Gilbreth's motion studies, standard work, and other important practices that form the bedrock of the industrial engineering methods used in kaizen and which, in turn, resulted in huge productivity improvements at Toyota that helped propel them to where they are today.

Taylor should be respected as much as Henry Ford and Taiichi Ohno. Here is why. Taylor came from a wealthy family, but instead of taking the easy path he became an apprentice patternmaker and machinist. He worked his way up from the shop floor to supervisor. So, from his years of experience in the shop, he knew well the machining trade, how workers worked, and how they sometimes did not work. It is there that Taylor began to develop his system of management – by getting his hands dirty on the shop floor and then putting his ideas into practice, via experimentation, in collaboration with the workers that he supervised.

What do Lean people value and respect in a person? Getting your hands dirty, knowing the job, doing experiments using the Scientific Method (and its derivative forms), collaborating with workers (teamwork). Taylor thought the shop floor was where learning took place and experiments were the best means by which problems could be solved. From there, Taylor worked his way up to become an executive. Later, Taylor and his steel company colleagues did years of careful experiments on the composition and heat treatment of tool steels, which led to an immensely useful invention called "high-speed steel."

The royalties from patents for high-speed steel made Taylor a wealthy man. Taylor was a pragmatic, fact-based person, skilled in engineering and experimentation, persuasive in getting people to try new things, an inventor, the developer of a comprehensive new system of progressive management based on the Scientific Method, and the father of industrial engineering. Lean people should take pride in Taylor and his work as it strengthens Lean management, not weakens it.

The high-speed steel invention and, later, the book *The Principles of Scientific Management*, made Taylor internationally famous. But it also earned him some unwanted notoriety. Managers in the U.S. who read his book adopted only pieces of Scientific Management, not the system in its entirety. Taylor's camp advocated for Real Scientific Management – "Betterment" and "Cooperation" – while business leaders adopted Fake Scientific Management. They were interested only in "Betterment." The widespread adoption of Fake

Scientific Management by managers in industry got Taylor into trouble.

Taylor was summoned to testify before a Congressional subcommittee in January of 1912 to explain the Taylor system. He did that, and also patiently and eloquently explained the difference between Fake Scientific Management and Real Scientific Management. Taylor's testimony provided many memorable quotes, including this one: "It ceases to be scientific management the moment it is used for bad." The same must be said about Lean management today.

Taylor's book, *The Principles of Scientific Management*, was translated into many languages, including Japanese, and was a very popular book in Japan. It was adopted by Japanese business leaders in the spirit that Taylor had practiced himself and which he had intended: Real Scientific Management ("Betterment" and "Cooperation"). The existence of Fake Scientific Management was far less prevalent in Japan than in the United States.

Judging Taylor's management system against the current standard, Toyota, as is commonly done, is thoughtless. Further, Taylor and Ohno were trying to solve different problems in different eras, through the methods for doing so had considerable overlap. Taylor faced a sellers' market while Ohno faced a buyers' market. Taylor was concerned about underproduction while Ohno was concerned about overproduction. Both Taylor and Ohno wanted lower-level people to make improvements based on facts instead of opinions – especially the opinions of people who had power ("the boss"). Both Taylor and Ohno wanted to improve productivity and reduce costs. And Both wanted to create what Ohno would later call the "full work system" [1].

When Taylor is vilified today, what is he vilified for? It is only two things. First, his approach to determining standards (standard work). He thought standards were best determined by an educated person (an engineer) specifically trained to do this type of job (i.e. time and motion study, with a stopwatch), and that there was "one best way" to do the work. The second was his view towards workers, which seemed harsh due to the words that Taylor used to describe workers in his writings and the manner in which they sometimes curtailed output, called "soldiering" (Ohno called it "waste;" i.e. waiting or idle time). So, despite the many benefits of the "Taylor system" compared to the conventional (zero-sum, win-lose) management practice of the day, it is these two things that people remember most and for which they vilify Taylor today. But is right to vilify him for these two things?

No, it is not, and here's why. In the early development of progressive management, Taylor's rationale for who should create standards was sensible and appropriate, and his view of workers was actually progressive for the times. It was far less harsh than the way most managers viewed both work and workers. In fact, Taylor's views on standards [2] and workers was revolutionary for the day and far more humane and remunerative than was typically the case. Further, Taylor's work evolved after his death in 1915 at the age of 59, to be more inclusive of worker input, and the "one best way" gave way to "continuous improvement." The flow production system created by Frank George Woollard (ca. 1925) in the U.K. [3], was influenced by both Taylor and Ford, and had as its principles, "Continuous Improvement" and "Benefit for All." The Toyota Way principles, "Continuous Improvement" and "Respect for People," are traceable back to Taylor's work.

To understand Taylor's view towards workers and society, it is helpful to read the 13-page paper, "The Spirit and Social Significance of Scientific Management" by Morris Cooke [4]. The most concise explanation of the controversies surrounding Taylor's work is found in a small, 103-page book titled, *Primer of Scientific Management* by Frank Gilbreth [2]. To clearly understand the difference between Real Scientific Management and Fake Scientific Management, read Taylor's lengthy January 1912 testimony to Congress [5]. Like Lean management, Scientific Management is difficult to comprehend, and those who don't study it carefully and thoroughly will surely misunderstand it as well as Taylor.

To understand Scientific Management, one has to read a large body of work, not solely Taylor's two papers "A Piece-Rate System" [6] and "Shop Management" [7], and his book *The Principles of Scientific Management* [8]. One must begin with works by the (mechanical) engineers that preceded Taylor (e.g. Henry Towne [9]), as well as the works written by Taylor's contemporaries – business owners, consultants, and academics. These include Morris Cooke, Frank Gilbreth, C. Bertrand Thompson, Henry Farquhar, Carl Barth, Horace Drury, Harlow Person, Henry Gantt, James Dodge, Henry Kendall, Horace Hathaway, Harrington Emerson, Charles Going, Dexter Kimball, Hugo Diemer, and so on, as well as the works by industrial engineers that followed them such as Ralph Barnes and George Shepard (principally in the 1930-1945 time-frame, and which includes Training Within Industry).

The poor understanding that the Lean producers and others have about Taylor and of Scientific Management suggests that they have done limited or poor research on this important topic. The job of advancing progressive Lean management is made far more difficult, and likely imperils the existence of Lean, if misconceptions about Scientific Management are allowed to persist. So it is in Lean movement's best interest to respect Taylor, to embrace Taylor, and to correct misunderstandings about him and his work. To do otherwise is to be a Lean hypocrite: respect some pioneers of progressive management while disrespecting others – and for reasons that are not fact-based.

Taylor possessed the characteristics valued by Lean people: Hard work, get your hands dirty, know the job, do experiments scientifically, be creative, collaborate with workers, and create better (non-zero-sum, win-win) outcomes for employees, customers, investors, and society at-large (i.e. humanity).

I am certain that Taylor, were he alive today, would be mystified at how people have remained stuck on two misinterpretations of his work (and Fake Scientific Management), the effort that people put into vilifying him, and how the great work of those who built on Taylor's work, from 1915 through the 1950s, is so poorly understood, both on its own and in relation to Toyota's management system.

Toyota did not invent their management system all by themselves. They built on the work of others and made many very important contributions for which their admiration and recognition are well-deserved. Taylor's work is part of the lineage of Toyota's management system and of Lean management as well.

Questions to consider:

- What different methods can be used to eliminate confusion that exists between Lean and Taylorism?
- Why is it so difficult to respect Taylor, his work, Scientific Management, or industrial engineering?
- Why is Taylor's work over 100 years ago judged against today's understanding of TPS and today's standards of conduct towards employees and business interests?
- Will Lean movement leaders acknowledge and correct their errors in interpreting Taylor's work for the sake of advancing Lean management?

Enduring Misunderstandings

This is a critique of selected passages from the article "Dealing with Lean's Crazy Relatives" by James P. Womack [10]. It reveals many misunderstandings about Frederick Winslow Taylor and his work.

Dealing with Lean's Crazy Relatives

Comment: That is a disrespectful title that blames people. It diminishes the important work of great contributors to the economic and social development of America, the creation of the discipline of industrial engineering, the science of process improvement, and modern industrial management. It ignores the fact that Taylor and Ford's work were necessary steps on the road to Toyota's Production System.

> Every family has a few members who are eccentric and problematic... crazy relatives can become a real problem if their antics reflect on the whole family. In the lean movement my two candidates for crazy relatives are Frederick Taylor and Henry Ford, who continue to cause us trouble 101 and 69 years after passing from this life.

Comment: This is a poor analogy, as mental health is nothing to joke about. Taylor and Ford are not the ones causing trouble to the Lean movement. There are many factors that contribute to the broad-based misunderstanding of Lean. These span social, economic, political, and historical factors [11]. The ills of Lean cannot rightly be attributed to two people, Taylor and Ford, as it is managers who struggle to put Lean (or any other challenging method) into practice, driven by preconceptions that they do not question or are unable to destroy.

> Frederick Taylor, most famous for *The Principles of Scientific Management* published in 1911, did one good thing – he focused on how people did their work... Taylor wanted to

change this by observing each job in an organization… to find out who performed the job the most effectively, what Taylor called "the one best way". He then wanted to standardize this practice and direct everyone else to follow it while setting a higher production target to qualify for a bonus. He believed that everyone could make the bonus by following his standard work and everyone would be better off.

Comment: Taylor did many good things, not just one. This includes working tirelessly to improve relations between management and workers, and to assure that workers received a "square deal" (non-zero-sum outcome). Literature from the 1910s and 1920s contain detailed examples of twenty or so of organizations that successfully "installed" Scientific Management – but never in its entirety, as Taylor saw it (about the same number of organizations today to practice TPS well). The "the one best way" was how Taylor conceptualized work standards, similar to Ohno's view that the standard is the least amount of time that it takes to do the work. Within about five years after Taylor's death, his followers began to speak of "continuous improvement" and "worker participation" in improvement. Thus, the "one best way" evolved.

What was wrong with Taylor's approach? Just about everything.

Comment: Incorrect. Taylor's work was the foundation upon which ideas and practices evolved. Large portions of Taylor's work (and Gilbreth and others) – industrial engineering – remain as the foundation of TPS (and kaizen). It is inappropriate and unfair to judge Taylor's thinking and actions then in today's context, which benefit from over 100 years of evolution in thinking and practice.

Taylor was convinced that most workers hated to work and were therefore "soldiering", pretending they were working as hard as they could. It was management's job to make them work harder and this required a sharp distinction between those doing the work and the managers thinking about how to get them to do the work. Thus the need for the manager to actually understand the work by observing the work.

Comment: Taylor knew about "soldiering" first-hand because he started as a machinist on the shop floor and worked his way up to become an executive. He viewed soldiering, which still exists today among both employees *and* managers, as greatly diminishing employer and employees' economic and non-economic interests. In Taylor's day, it made sense for an educated person to figure out how people should work – not a manager, but an engineer. Recognize that in the late 1800s, some 90 percent of the U.S. population had less than a high school education, and therefore the English literacy and numeracy rate was very low by today's standard. Taylor had the progressive view that management's job was to make the work easier, not harder, with the help of engineers observing the work and identifying better methods for workers to try.

This meant in practice that the person doing the work the "best" way would effectively have his knowledge appropriated for use by everyone else without any reward. And everyone else would be mindlessly and grumpily following the instructions of the manager-expert based on the best way of the best worker. A great formula for mass misery.

Comment: The "best" way of doing the work was merely an alternate expression, then, for the word "standard." In TPS, standards remain of fundamental importance. "Mass misery" was not the result in organizations where Taylor's system was "installed" properly. It was the result in organizations where Taylor's system was misunderstood and installed improperly [12].

But Taylor didn't stop there. He envisioned the work needed to create a completed product as a set of isolated, discrete steps, not as a continuous flow.

Comment: This is true. But implicit in Womack's criticism is that Taylor should have figured that work should be made to flow continuously. At the time, the need for flow did not exist because most markets for manufactured goods were sellers' markets, so batch-and-queue processing and supporting systems made perfect sense. Taylor did his part, and others who followed (Ford *et al.*) built upon his work which resulted in continuous flow (in final assembly, but not in upstream processes. An exception was engine manufacturing at Morris Motors in the U.K. [3]).

So there was no need to align and tightly connect all of the work with everyone working at the same rate (known to us today as takt time.)

Comment: Frank George Woollard (1883-1957) [3], who built on Ford's and Taylor's work, paced work according to a takt time in the U.K. automotive industry in the 1920s.

He concluded that process village layouts were fine if progress was monitored with accurate "travelers" and production schedules for each step (later automated as MRP) and that the really important task for managers was to make full use of the assets in each village, both technical and human. This led to chronic overproduction to keep every machine and worker busy.

Comment: This was the right thing to do back then (1880s through the 1930s) because it was a sellers' market. So, in general, batch-and-queue processing and overproduction were sensible practices. When markets go from sellers' to buyer's, batch-and-queue production and overproduction then cause many problems. The transition to buyers' markets started to occur in the U.S. in the 1930s and in Japan after World War II.

To make the best of a bad thing, Taylor also invented standard-cost, absorption accounting, which judged managers on how fully they utilized labor and machines and then treated in-process inventories, no matter how unnecessary, as assets.

Comment: Taylor did not invent standard cost absorption accounting. That distinction belongs to G. Charter Harrison [13]. It was invented in relation to the sellers' markets that existed at the time. It was an effective way to account for costs when using the batch-and-queue production method.

As for improvement beyond current best practice, this was to be done by experts making observations without consultation with workers or line managers and, in Taylor's case, by external consultants. Indeed, Taylor invented the modern consulting industry as the first management consultant, in addition to being the first process consultant.

Comment: As noted earlier, in Taylor's day it made sense for experts (engineers) to think of new and better methods. But this approach changed soon after Taylor's death. Yes, Taylor invented the modern management consulting industry. But, it's worth noting the difference between Taylor's consulting work (virtuous and financially unsuccessful) and that of amazingly successful "charlatans" and "fakirs" such as Charles Bedaux (1886-1944) [14].

Oh, and finally, Taylor was a notorious cheat who doctored his results regarding productivity gains... Good grief. A really bad relative.

Comment: Irrespective of doctoring results, Taylor's invention – industrial engineering – is the basis for kaizen and has proven successful in dramatically improving productivity. In the right hands, and with the right mindset, industrial engineering also improves worker's lives and their economic condition.

> Henry Ford had no use for Taylor… in the early days, until the Highland Park complex was completed in 1914, Ford's line managers and workers consulted intensively about the best way to do each task in Ford's new flow production system by working backwards from the work itself, not by observing many workers to see who did the work the best way. But as his company grew in size, managers began to simply tell workers what to do and how to improve their work based on the analysis of industrial engineers. Workers were to keep their heads down and keep working – Taylor had come in through the back door.

Comment: It is not Taylor who had "come through the back door." Managers telling workers what to do pre-dates Taylor by thousands of years.

> Today, we suffer from Taylor and Ford when critics rely on pattern recognition to brand us as "Taylorists" or "Fordists", always focusing on the issue of work design and management. They see one dimension of one small piece of lean's tool kit – standardizing individual jobs – as the whole.

Comment: As noted in "Selective Adoration," Womack would be wise to embrace Taylor, despite any professional or personal imperfections, rather than run away from Taylor – which is likely impossible to do anyway.

> The lean movement over 100 years has moved a long ways beyond our crazy American relatives, Taylor and Ford, by going to Japan and back and by adapting lean principles to practically every type of value-creating activity across the world. So let's invite our critics to come along with us,

beyond simple pattern recognition and kneejerk responses to the very notion of standardized work, to a higher level of understanding about the nature of human work and how to it make better.

Comment: The Lean movement has not existed for over 100 years. It has existed for about 30 years (1988-2017) [15]. The progressive management movement has existed on-and-off for about 127 years (1890-2017) [9]. The birth of Lean is not the same as the birth of TPS [16], which dates to about 1947 [1].

Ultimately, Womack's article fails to put distance between Lean and its antecedents, and does not overcome one common source of resistance to Lean – Taylor – nor does it address the dozens of other sources of resistance [11]. Womack succeeds only in further advancing misconceptions and mischaracterizations about Taylor and his work, rather than eliminating them.

In terms of their professional work, Taylor and Ford were not crazy. Far from it. They worked diligently, over many years, to solve the most pressing problems in industrial management of the day. And we are following in their footsteps whether we like it or not.

Finally, if Womack's true objective is to separate Lean from Taylor, then he must also separate Lean from Toyota.

Questions to consider:

- Why are Toyota people's efforts held in so much higher regard than Scientific Management people's efforts, given that the former is in large part the product of the latter?
- Why are the facts about Taylor's work and times so difficult for others to accurately grasp?

- What benefit does Womack or Lean gain from disparaging Taylor, his work, Scientific Management, or industrial engineering?
- Does disparaging Taylor, his work, Scientific Management, or industrial engineering enhance or reduce the credibility of Lean and its producers?
- Womack's byline in Planet Lean (www.planet-lean.com) articles characterize him this way: "Management expert James P. Womack, is the founder and senior advisor to the Lean Enterprise Institute." As a self-proclaimed expert, Womack criticizes management experts (industrial engineers) in Taylor's day for specifying how workers should do their work. Doesn't Womack do exactly the same thing? Is it hypocrisy? Or is it nothing more than the universal curse suffered by those who know much about a given subject?

Just-Too-Late

2014 was the year that the "Respect for People" principle finally gained traction in the Lean community. It took a long for this to happen because the producers of Lean seem to have ignored "Respect for People" for many years and apparently did not comprehend the critical role it plays in the proper functioning of TPS. This can be attributed to one or more of the following:

- A lack of first-hand experience with TPS
- Simple misunderstandings
- Incomplete research
- Biased research

Whatever the cause, opportunities to help people correctly comprehend Lean management were lost for over 25 years – a critical period of time for business and for workers in economically advanced nations.

In January of 2008, James P. Womack wrote an article for *Reliable Plant* titled, "The Toyota concept of 'respect for people" In it he said [17]:

> "When in recent years Toyota made respect for people one of the pillars of the Toyota Way…"

That bit of a sentence shows a stunning lack of awareness of the "Respect for People" principle in Toyota's management practice and the process by which the The Toyota Way 2001 document was created [18].

Careful study the history of Toyota Motor Corporation, Toyota management's mindset and practices, and the evolution of Toyota's production system (and of progressive management itself) should have clearly revealed that "Respect for People" was not a recent addition to The Toyota Way.

Toyota describes the creation of "The Toyota Way 2001" document as follows [19]:

"...in October 1998, TMC established the Toyota Way Compilation Project Secretariat inside the BR Global Human Resources Department and set out to compile the Toyota Way. The Toyota Way gathered together the management philosophy and values that had been passed on as implicit knowledge and made them available in an easy-to-understand systematic and visual manner...

For this project, the philosophies and values of predecessors and forbearers were extracted from the Toyoda Precepts and the Guiding Principles at Toyota and, following many rounds of consultation with TMC executives, were compiled as the Toyota Way 2001 in April 2001. This document explained the five key concepts of 'Challenge', 'Kaizen (continuous improvement)', 'Genchi Genbutsu (go to the source to find the facts)', 'Respect', and 'Teamwork', under the two main principles of 'Continuous Improvement' and 'Respect for People'..."

This information has been on Toyota's web site for many years.

The Toyota Way was around for a long time and finally codified in printed form in April 2001. The existence of the "Respect for People" principle was no secret. It could be found in the writings and speeches of former executives, in their decision-making, and in the early accounts and studies of Toyota's production system. For example:

In the 1977 paper by "Toyota Production System and Kanban System: Materialization of Just-In-Time and Respect-For-Human System," Sugimori *et al.* said [20]:

"Toyota firmly believes that making up a system where the capable Japanese workers can actively participate in running and improving their workshops and be able to fully display their capabilities would be foundation of human respect environment of the highest order."

In the 1983 book *Toyota Production System: Practical Approach to Production Management,* Monden said this about sub-goal three [21]:

"3. Respect-for-humanity, which must be cultivated while the system utilizes the human resources to obtain its cost objectives."

And that:

"...these three goals cannot exist independently or be achieved independently without influencing each other or the primary goal of cost reduction. It is a special feature of the Toyota production system that the primary goal cannot be achieved without realization of the subgoals and vice versa."

In the 1988 book *Toyota Production System: Beyond Large Scale Production,* Ohno said (italics added) [22]:

"The most important objective of the Toyota system has been to increase production efficiency by constantly and thoroughly eliminating waste. This concept, and *the equally important respect for humanity* that has passed down from the venerable Toyoda Sakichi (1867-1930), founder of the company and master of inventions, to his son Toyoda Kiichiro (1894-1952), Toyota Motor Company's first president and father of the Japanese passenger car, are the foundation of the Toyota production system." (italics added).

Fujio Cho, former president and chairman of Toyota Motor Corporation said [23]:

> "The philosophy that makes [continuous improvement] possible is 'Respect for People'."

Given that "Respect for People" enables continuous improvement, discounting or ignoring the "Respect for People" principle is a fundamental error in comprehending Toyota's production system, as well as the history of progressive management.

Lean clearly did not conform to the progressive management standard, "Continuous Improvement" and "Respect for People" (and variants of these as progressive management evolved over time). Lean left out "Respect for People" and, by doing so, did not respect people.

But this is more than just a fundamental error. Lean contained a serious design defect the moment it was introduced to the public 1988, when the goal of improving material and information flow was decoupled from "Respect for People." For 20 years thereafter, the producers of Lean, Womack and Jones, and many others, advanced a management practice whose main element for success – and its most distinctive feature – was missing.

The book *Lean Thinking* was presented to the public as a way to create corporate wealth for owners and investors. The consequence of that positioning and of leaving out the "Respect for People" principle was, in some measure, that large numbers of people were laid off as a result of Lean.

That zero-sum outcome is easily predictable given the 100-plus year history of progressive management Ignoring the "Respect for People" for two decades could not have come at a worse time for workers and their families. For them, any correction now made by the producers of Lean is just-too-late.

Remarkably, the producers of Lean fail to acknowledge the harm done in anything other than a token way. They have simply moved on and started to vigorously promote "Respect for People." Perhaps it is better late than never. But, it is certain that a long-term effort is needed to correct business leaders' understanding and practice of Lean management, and teach them that wealth creation is a by-product of progressive management, not its objective.

Questions to consider:

• Can business leaders' understanding and practice of Lean now be corrected?
• What methods can be used to teach business leaders about "Respect for People?"
• Do leaders care about "Respect for People," even if they are educated on the topic?
• Is it too late? Are business leaders more interested in technology; replacing labor with robots and artificial intelligence?
• What is the future of Lean as business leaders' interests shift to technology and artificial intelligence?
• Did Lean miss the biggest opportunity, perhaps ever, to change business leaders' thinking about the value and capabilities of humans who are engaged in value-creating work?

Still Missing the Point

The Lean Enterprise Institute's Lean Transformation Framework encompasses five questions [24]. The first question is: "What problem are we trying to solve?" For most people, it is a reasonable first question to ask. But there are two other important related questions:

1. Who should answer that first question?
2. Is there a common answer?

In LEIs Lean Transformation Framework, it seems that everyone should answer that first question and that there is no common answer for organizations. The question is open-ended and so too will be the answer depending on who answers it; anyone from CEO to shop floor associate.

For this reason, LEIs Lean Transformation Framework seems to me more likely to generate large amounts of Lean "busywork" than produce major business results. Allow me to explain this iconoclastic point of view:

The context, Lean transformation, reflects changes in mindset and practices across an entire organization. Given the scope of change, the first question can only be answered by the executive team. After all, Lean, we are now told, is a strategy, and so executives are clearly responsible for answering this first question for an organization. Given what concerns CEOs, the answer will surely be specific and connected to actual business needs. One such need that all businesses have, and which all CEOs care about, is cost reduction. So, the question "What problem are we trying to solve?" can yield a common answer both within a business or for any business: cost reduction. There are many methods to achieve cost reduction. However, executives should seek methods that strengthen competitiveness, not weaken it. Strengthening competitiveness means finding methods to reduce costs when production volumes are low. Simply increasing production quantities to reduce costs (i.e. economies of scale), which anyone can do, weakens competitiveness in buyers' markets.

While the first question must cascade through the organization, so too must its answer in order to focus team and individual problem-solving efforts. If not, then people will be busy solving problems for which there is no actual business need. This is called "busy work," which we have all experienced. If employees continue the same old pattern of doing "busy work" while under LEI's Lean Transformation Framework, then people will work to solve problems that have no business need and produce no business result. And there will be no Lean transformation.

Most businesses operate in competitive (buyers') markets. Daily competition and the existence of other threats to survival means a business cannot afford to solve problems disconnected from actual needs and which have no business impact. It wastes time and resources, and will put them further and further behind the competition as time goes by. It also wastes people's (employees') lives.

For Taiichi Ohno, the answer to the question "What problem are we trying to solve?" was not ambiguous or open-ended. It was specific and reflected actual needs as perceived by Toyota's top leaders in their struggle to compete against Ford and General Motors' products in Japan, their competitors' cost-reduction efforts, customers' never-ending desire to pay less for improved products over time, the need to generate profits, and survival. In his book, *Toyota Production System*, Ohno clearly articulated the specific problem he was trying to solve:

> "Our problem was how to cut costs while producing small numbers of many types of cars." (p. 1)

What was the business need? The business need was the changing market that Toyota faced:

> "… [a] marketplace [that] required the production
> of small quantities of many varieties under
> conditions of low demand…" (p. xiii)

This, in turn, required the creation of a production system responsive to Japan's market conditions (buyers' market) so that Toyota could:

> "…make products that differ according to
> individual requirements…" (p. xiv)

The image below shows the logic that drove Toyota's transformation process. Should your logic be any different?

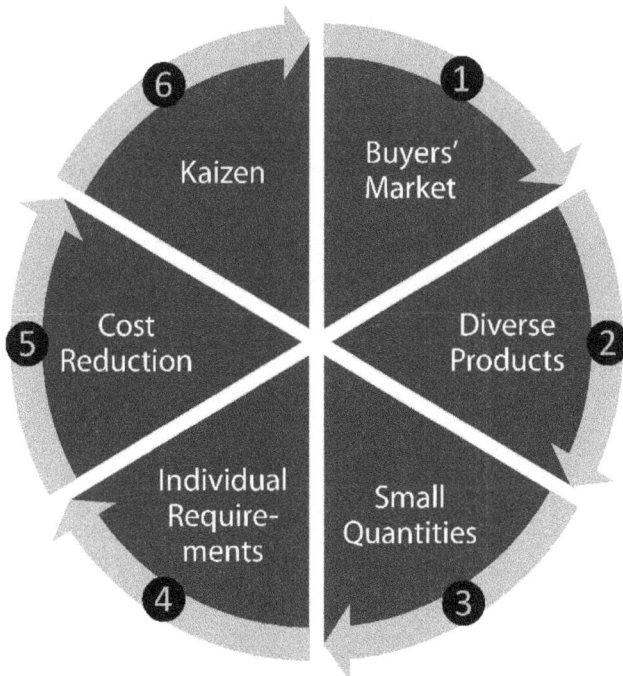

Toyota's transformation was the change from batch-and-queue production to flow, to satisfy customers. And, of course, the transformation affected all other parts of the business as well. That is why Ohno said:

> "…[it] means nothing less than adopting the Toyota production system as the management system of the whole company." (p. 41)

LEIs Lean Transformation Framework says that you should take a "situational approach." It says every situation unique and every countermeasure unique. It that true? In reality, your business environment, your problem, and your customers' desires are the same as what Toyota faced in the late 1940s and still faces in 2017. Therefore, you need to figure out how to reduce costs while producing small numbers of many types of products. How will you do that? You must change from batch-and-queue to flow, and transform all other parts of the business to support that. A situational approach? For most businesses, that is nonsense.

But it is not just changes in processes throughout the company. It is also changes in mindset for both management and workers. The change in mindset – what Ohno called "a revolution in consciousness" (p. 14) – is especially difficult for managers because it encompasses numerous economic, social, political, and historical factors that serve as powerful bulwarks against changes in thinking (as well as recognizing simple realities such as buyers' markets). This is why most Lean transformations fail, notwithstanding the ubiquity of Lean "busy work" and the lack of business results.

The change in manager's mindset has proven to be the greatest challenge over the course of the 125-year history of progressive management. For example, when Ohno said "cut costs," the conventional-mindset manager, whether in 1917 or 2017, immediately jumps to the idea of reducing headcount through layoffs. Hence, people today widely associate Lean with layoffs. But, Ohno never meant layoffs. He meant cutting costs in ways that did not harm people. In fact, he wanted people to benefit from the challenge and experience of participating in cost-cutting. How? By developing human capabilities; using their creativity and resourcefulness through hands-on and brain-on engagement in what he called "rationalization." What Ohno meant by "rationalization" was "kaizen" – Toyota's industrial engineering-based kaizen methods – to improve processes and the work, thereby improving productivity and cutting costs, while simultaneously satisfying customers and generating profit. This is why Taiichi Ohno stressed "the equally important respect for humanity" (p. xiii) in efforts to create and sustain the transformation.

Ohno said:

> "I wanted to illustrate how it [TPS] reduces costs by improving productivity with human effort and innovation [kaizen] even in periods of severe low growth – not by increasing quantities." (p. 119)

For every business that operates in a competitive environment – which is most businesses, whether for-profit or not-for-profit – the problem you are trying to solve today is virtually the same problem that Ohno and his team worked to solve over a 30-year period beginning in 1947. The situation is the same. The countermeasure is the same. And the process is the same.

> "The Toyota production system, however, is not just a production system. I am confident it will reveal its strength as a management system adapted to today's era of global markets…" (p. xv)

But, given that there are large differences between Lean transformation and Toyota transformation, you must make a choice: Lean transformation (ambiguous and   open-ended, devoid of kaizen and other important umami), or Toyota transformation. Choose the former and you will increase the risk of losing ground to competitors. Choose the latter and not only will you work towards solving Ohno's problem, you will instill organizational commitment and discipline to customer satisfaction.

Questions to consider:

- Does a "situational approach" clarify the challenge of Lean transformation? Or does it confuse it?
- Why was the driver of Toyota's transformation, market conditions, not clearly represented in Lean?
- What should you do if half your business serves buyers' markets and the other half serves sellers' markets? Is transformation right for you? Why or why not?
- What should you do if all of your business serves sellers' market? Is transformation right for you? Why or why not?
- If all of your business serves sellers' market, how would transformation benefit the business and its stakeholders in the long-run?

• • • • •

Note: When Ohno says "costs," he is referring to anything that directly or indirectly creates or reduces cost, whether it is measurable or not, and whether it is visible or not. So, "costs" means: productivity, hiring, training, work, work signals, work standards, work sequence, machines, tooling, maintenance, queue time, set-up time, part-travel time, cycle time, lead-time, space, materials, consumables, inventories, taxes, warehouses, energy, abnormal conditions, demand, parts, waste, unevenness, unreasonableness, spirit, challenge, creativity, innovation, teamwork, learning, evolution... and a thousand more things. If you rely solely on budgets and spreadsheets as your indicators of costs, then you will never understand TPS.

5

What Next?

The Long View

2017 is the 20th anniversary of the founding of the Lean Enterprise Institute. It is an organization that has inarguably been the most successful and influential in shaping people's understanding of "lean," due in part to the central role that its founder, James P. Womack, and his associate, Daniel T. Jones of the Lean Enterprise Academy (U.K.), have played in bringing it into our collective consciousness.

What follows is a personal reflection on this important period of time during which Lean grew immensely in popularity. It includes a look back to the past, through to the present, and into the future of Lean.

Preamble

More than 30 years ago, Taiichi Ohno warned [1]:

> "...those who decide to implement the Toyota production system must be fully committed. If you try to adopt only the 'good parts', you'll fail."

Think about these two questions as you read on:

- Is Lean, in fact, "only the good parts" of Toyota's production system? If so, then it clearly sets people up to fail. Does that respect people [2]?

- Were the producers who gave us "lean" under the pretext as being synonymous with Toyota's production system beginning in 1988, and today as synonymous with TPS and The Toyota Way, truly committed to adopting all the parts (mindset and methods), not "only the good parts?"

The Past

Twenty years ago, I was a great admirer of LEI. I had high hopes that it would bring a lot of good to the business world – for all stakeholders, but especially to employees. And in some measure it has. There are many examples of organizations that, to varying degrees, made improvements over time which resulted in better outcomes for employees, suppliers, customers, investors, and communities. Through Womack and Jones's efforts, the world learned of their interpretation of Toyota's production system, Lean production from 1988 to 2008, and Lean management since then.

But my admiration for LEI quickly faded. Why? I felt that LEI had fallen behind soon after it was formed. TPS and Lean, while originally said to be the same, are actually very different, and the gap between the two widened over time as I learned more about TPS, as well as Toyota's overall management system. I could clearly see a narrow focus on tools and that major elements were missing in Lean, resulting in the potential for managers to do harm to employees in the organizations that adopted it. Too often, harm actually did occur. That bothered me, but it did not appear that that Womack and Jones were bothered.

Let's be clear: Harm done to employees or other stakeholder is an abnormal condition. The normal condition is no harm, mutual benefit, and mutual prosperity, just as the critics of classical economics had argued (see Chapter 3, "How Economics Subverts Lean"). This was not business leaders' view of workers and their work 29 years ago when Lean first came to us in 1988 or when organizations such as LEI and LEA were later formed.

Therefore, efforts must be fully directed towards helping leaders and organizations understand and achieve the normal condition. That includes accurate representations of what

Toyota's management system is – mindset (especially), as well as methods – understanding in detail why some organizations succeed, and meticulous root cause analysis of organizations that failed in their Lean transformation process – of which there are many to study.

My criticisms of Lean have been many and varied, but several of the criticisms can be summed up this way: *Slowness to recognize new, relevant information and slowness to take action based on the new information.* For example, the "Respect for People" principle, which is essential for the proper functioning of TPS [3], has been evident throughout the long history of progressive management. This omission, long in duration, damaged the Lean brand.

But more importantly, it caused pain and suffering to employees in organizations where managers used Lean improve productivity so that they could cut labor costs by firing employees. The absence of the "Respect for People" principle for so many years gave business leaders permission to do harm to people under the name of Lean. The long silence from the global leaders of the Lean movement was astounding.

It is not the job of managers to cause human suffering. And it is not the job of any promoter of Lean to cause or contribute to human suffering. But that is what happened for twenty or more years.

A similar situation existed for leadership. It is again clear from the long history of progressive management that leadership plays a critically important role in the transition from supply-driven batch-and-queue conventional management to demand-driven TPS (flow). And, the depth and breadth to which leaders must change encompasses a wide range of beliefs, behaviors, knowledge, and practices pertaining to both people and business – economic, social, and political – as well as the differences between batch-and-queue processing and flow, and how to successfully transition from one to the other. These aspects have long been underappreciated by LEI/LEA, if even recognized.

Lateness in changing from Lean production to Lean management, lateness in recognizing the "Respect for People" principle, lateness in understanding the importance of leadership as well as the detailed differences between conventional leaders and Lean leaders, and lateness in studying and learning the root causes Lean transformation process failures. The information was out there, easily found and ready-made for distribution to eager and highly committed followers of Lean. This would have helped people closer to the time in which they actually needed the information. It surely would have averted harm to some people. And it would have averted harm to the Lean brand.

The Present

I teach a graduate course in which students analyze various types of product, process, and business failures using the A4 method that I developed starting in 2004. LEI reminds me of one case in particular that we studied several times. That of Microsoft.

For decades, Microsoft's success was largely due to its monopoly position in its primary marketplaces – operating systems and office software. Under the leadership of Bill Gates and Steve Ballmer, Microsoft achieved impressive gains in sales growth and profits. It succeeded in certain quantitative business metrics, but it failed in other areas that were less easy to measure.

Microsoft was a Windows-centric organization under Gates and Ballmer; everything must be about Windows, all the time. Every product and service must connect to Windows – even if it displeased customers. A similar dynamic seems to have long existed at LEI (and LEA as well) with respect to Lean.

Microsoft did not listen to outsiders or critics. It listened only to insiders, and especially those who were with the company for many years. It became insular, suffered from the not-invented-here syndrome, and thus missed many new opportunities to respond to and better satisfy customers. And it had difficulty learning from others. A similar dynamic seems to have long existed at LEI with respect to listening and learning.

Microsoft was good at buying technology from others and often did a good job of internally developing the product further, but it was poor at developing its own new products. Microsoft was slow to adapt and evolve as times changed. A similar dynamic seems to have long existed at LEI (and LEA as well) with respect to Lean.

In recent years, Microsoft's new CEO, Satya Nadella, eliminated the need for everything Microsoft does to be Windows-centric. He has invited outsiders and critics, to learn from them, and embracing things invented elsewhere as well as the people who invented them – including open-source software. Microsoft is now better able to adapt to changing conditions, innovate, and survive.

While Toyota has been and remains a great source of inspiration, ideas, and practices, they are not the only people or organization that LEI and LEA can learn from. LEIs and LEAs constituents want information and training that will help them succeed in their particular circumstances, delivered in a timely manner, regardless of its origin – especially in the areas where LEI and LEA have historically been weak: Kaizen, leadership, "Respect for People," and detailed analyses of Lean success and failure.

Windows remains a closed-source (proprietary) software system. TPS is akin to that; it is a closed-source management system. While there is sharing of some pieces of the source code, Toyota is under no obligation to share the entire code. Lean was presented to us in the past as a generic equivalent to TPS, and in the present as the generic equivalent of Toyota's management system. Unfortunately, Lean has, for decades, been a far more closed-source management system than open-source – though, being "generic," it should have been an open-source progressive management system from the start that everyone could contribute to and improve.

As de facto gatekeeper for Lean and its MIT origins, major contributions from numerous sources, including Toyota, seem to have been purposefully excluded. For decades, large and important chunks of code were missing from LEI/LEAs interpretation of TPS despite its easy availability. This had a great effect on people and on outcomes.

The Future

In order for LEI achieve its mission, "Make things better, through lean thinking and practice," it must gather up the useful pieces of code that exist at any point in time – past, present, and future – and incorporate them into a new open-source Lean management system. The future of Lean is to generalize its applicability into new and relevant domains that satisfy the needs of organizations.

Fundamentally, TPS, upon which Toyota's management system is based, is a human information processing system. It is a solution for information flow problems between humans within and between organizations, and also between humans and machines. This generalized feature is extremely important because blocked information flows cause innumerable problems for people, organizations, and society. Lean must be significantly upgraded to gain similar functionality to TPS and The Toyota Way as a human information processing system.

And it should allow others to contribute to the source code so that Lean can evolve into a system for improving human health in organizations. This evolutionary direction gives business leaders an additional substantive reason to adopt Lean management and to learn how to practice it with distinction. Perhaps someday employees leave work healthier than when they arrived.

Lean as a solution for information flow problems and as a system for improving human health can evolve over time in series, or perhaps even in parallel. However, past errors must not be repeated in the presentation, promotion, and advancement of Lean. Lean must do good things for people and be unambiguously recognized for the good that it does. If Lean evolves in a way that continues to cause harm to people, then Lean will soon fade away.

Re-positioning Lean this way will require effort to change long-established negative perceptions of Lean. But, moving Lean into this new direction will challenge people to think anew of what Lean really is. If Lean management evolves quickly in ways that are recognized as beneficial to both business and humanity, then it may survive long-term. The image on the following page depicts a life cycle that Lean may be subject to if it does not evolve.

Lean could be on the cusp of being overtaken by digital transformation, a new technology that business leaders are sure to rapidly adopt. While Lean management should be complimentary to digital business transformation, senior executives may not see it that way. They may use digital transformation as a justification to move away from Lean transformation, which they have clearly struggled to with both personally (i.e. practice and learning) and organizationally (i.e. transformation).

Lean Management Life Cycle

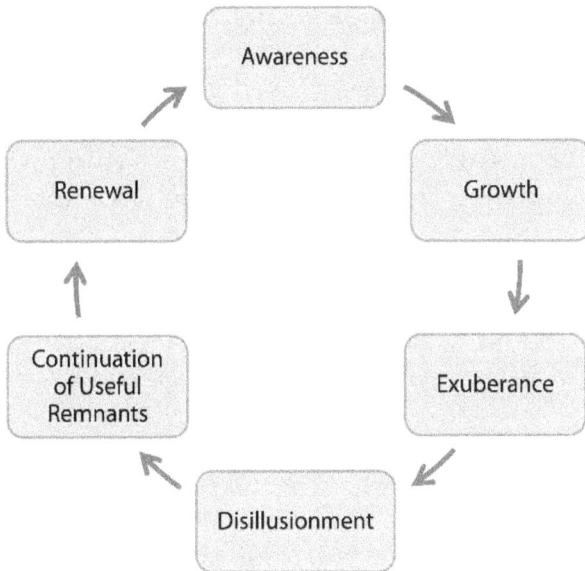

```
                    ┌─────────────┐
              ↗     │  Awareness  │    ↘
    ┌─────────────┐ └─────────────┘ ┌─────────────┐
    │   Renewal   │                 │   Growth    │
    └─────────────┘                 └─────────────┘
         ↑                                 ↓
┌─────────────┐                     ┌─────────────┐
│ Continuation│                     │  Exuberance │
│  of Useful  │                     └─────────────┘
│  Remnants   │    ↖             ↙
└─────────────┘    ┌─────────────────┐
                   │ Disillusionment │
                   └─────────────────┘
```

In a digital world, the survival of Lean management, and Toyota kaizen methods in particular, seems essential because it will help assure that people remain connected to the authentic, tactile, and value-laden human experiences of teamwork and seeking to continuously improve. But things might not turn out that way.

Artificial intelligence (AI) and other technologies are rapidly capturing business leaders' interests and investments. It will become an important element of decision-making, if not the decision-maker. To fulfill that role, AI will learn all that is known about classical and neoclassical economics, supply-driven sellers' markets, the batch-and-queue production method, and related knowledge. If that happens, then Lean is unlikely to survive because the fountain of knowledge that people trust, AI, will know little about Lean or judge Lean to be unimportant. The algorithm will decide conventional management is best for business and for humanity.

Alternatively, if we teach AI about TPS (inclusive of product development, supplier and dealer networks), perhaps it will comprehend the inadequacy of classical and neoclassical economics, supply-driven sellers' markets, the batch-and-queue production method, and related knowledge. Perhaps AI will be the decision-maker that informs business leaders (or other AI agents) of the superiority of TPS economics; demand-driven buyers' markets, flow, and related knowledge. In this scenario, the algorithm will decide progressive management is better for business and for humanity. And people would determine how to improve progressive management though kaizen.

It would remarkable if someday an algorithm made better judgments than humans (economists, politicians, business leaders, academics, etc.) about how to balance the interests of capital and labor. The 250-year battle would finally be over – or at least reduced to occasional skirmishes.

Questions to consider:

- Is Lean, in fact, "only the good parts" of Toyota's production system? Did Lean set people up to fail? Did that respect people [2]?
- Were, or are, the producers who gave us "lean" under the pretext as being synonymous with Toyota's production system beginning in 1988, and today as synonymous with TPS and The Toyota Way, truly committed to adopting all the parts (mindset and methods), not "only the good parts?"
- Does Lean have a future if it remains closed-source?

- As an open-source management system, would Lean continue evolving in a progressive direction, or regress to conventional management given its ubiquity?
- What rules would have to be put in place to assure that Lean, as an open-source management system, evolves in a progressive direction and does not regress to conventional management?
- How could AI be taught TPS and The Toyota Way without directly experiencing it?
- Would the non-intuitive nature of TPS and The Toyota Way confound AI?
- Classical and neoclassical economics, supply-driven sellers' markets, the batch-and-queue production method, and related knowledge are all easily expressed by mathematical equations. However, the TPS economics, demand-driven buyers' markets, flow, and related knowledge, are not easily expressed by mathematical equations. How will that effect machine learning and decision-making?

Improving Lean Transformation Process

Given what we have learned about Lean transformation success and failure – what to do and what not to do – how should the leaders of an organization introduce Lean? And how can they do that in a way that inspires people to want to learn about progressive management principles and practices?

Lean is usually introduced by company presidents in non-inspiring ways. They start by dryly articulating business needs, followed immediately by a high-level explanation of a few technical elements, and then introduce the implementation plan. They leave out the social details, believing them to be unimportant. Call this the "Lean for Owners" method, which leaves workers suspicious of management's intentions. Introducing Lean this way does not respect workers and requires them to follow a leader who knows nothing about Lean. Decades of experience clearly informs us that the "Lean for Owners" method of introducing Lean is a loser.

Instead, consider reversing the process, addressing the social details first and the technical and business details last. In other words, present Lean from the workers' perspective, not from management's perspective. After all, workers are the customers of the management practice. Call this the "Lean for Workers" method. Introduce Lean in a patient, step-wise fashion, allowing time for workers to comprehend the upcoming changes in thinking and daily routine that are being asked of them. In this way, workers are respected. This is a smarter way to start.

Introduce Lean in four steps over a period of three months or so, carefully preparing the ground for acceptance. Focus each step on inspiring workers to believe in themselves and their capabilities for doing things that they never thought they could do. Emphasize inspiration in each step of the introduction to create demand for Lean by workers, rather than letting workers think that Lean is being forced onto them by management.

Pre-Work: In order to introduce Lean accurately and to be able to answer workers' questions, top managers should spend a few months doing some homework. They should learn about Lean from various sources, focusing intently on social aspects, flow, and kaizen. Leaders should participate in at least one shop floor kaizen whose objective is to create flow. This learn-by-doing will enable leaders to explain the kaizen process (and features related to *time*, such as the time from idea-to-test-to-practice), desired social and technical outcomes, and the nuances and details that workers will no doubt ask them about.

Week 1: Vividly describe what a better life at work can look like for workers. It would include simplification of the job, better safety, less stress, fewer errors, better relationships among workers and managers, growth of skills, higher pay, improved financial and non-financial results, and so on. Briefly describe how managers will think and do things differently to help realize a better life for workers, and commit to workers that nobody will be fired as a result of process improvement. Then, roam the workplace for many hours each day for the next week or two to answer questions that workers have, preferably one-by-one.

Week 3: Introduce the fundamental objective of Lean: Material and information flow. Describe a few key differences between the current processing method, batch-and-queue, and flow. Then, roam the workplace for many hours each day for the next week or two to answer questions that workers have, preferably one-by-one.

Week 5: Introduce the process for creating a Lean organization: Kaizen. Explain, in some detail, Toyota-style, industrial engineering-based kaizen. Focus on how kaizen is good for people; how it stimulates thinking and generates ideas, and is a fun activity because it engages people to be creative and innovative. Then, roam the workplace for many hours each day for the next week or two to answer questions that workers have, preferably one-by-one.

Week 7: Introduce the business need for kaizen, and reinforce the tight link between how kaizen helps grow both people and the business. Explain the kaizen process; what to expect, roles and responsibilities, expected outcomes. Explain the buyers' market that you face, how kaizen helps an organization respond to this type of market (shorter lead-time, lower costs, better quality, etc.), and management's vision for growth of success. Then, roam the workplace for many hours each day for the next week or two to answer questions that workers have, preferably one-by-one.

Week 9 and Forever After: Kaizen, followed by kaizen, kaizen, kaizen, kaizen, kaizen, kaizen… lots of kaizen led by highly capable facilitators. Managers must participate in kaizen as team members, not in their role as managers, and exhibit enthusiasm for what they and workers have learned and accomplished. Then, follow-up with workers post-kaizen to understand their experience, quickly share and apply learnings elsewhere in the organization, identify other processes to improve, identify opportunities to improve the kaizen process itself, and so on – preferably one-by-one.

Questions to consider:

- If an organization's Lean transformation process follows the same path as everyone else ("Lean for Owners"), can one expect different results or the same results?
- It is possible to succeed with Lean if management is not engaged in leaning Lean and therefore and does not know how to coach people?

- Besides the pre-work, what other preparations could managers make to create demand for Lean among workers ("Lean for Workers")?
- What standard work can managers engage in to keep the inspiration alive in future years?

Lean Transformation Models

Sometimes it is useful to follow a model for Lean transformation to visualize the challenge and to guide one's efforts. While there are dozens of Lean transformation models, the three models presented here should be particularly helpful:

- A change-over model
- An improved model based on the one promoted by the Lean Enterprise Institute [3]
- Model based on 3P (Production Preparation Process)

No Lean transformation visual model is perfect; they are simply representations of how to think and what to do, accurate to greater or lesser extents.

Change-Over Model

In 2003, I introduced what may have been the first Lean transformation model [4] describing how leaders could execute the change-over from conventional management to Lean management. It is based on the well-known method for machine changeover [5].

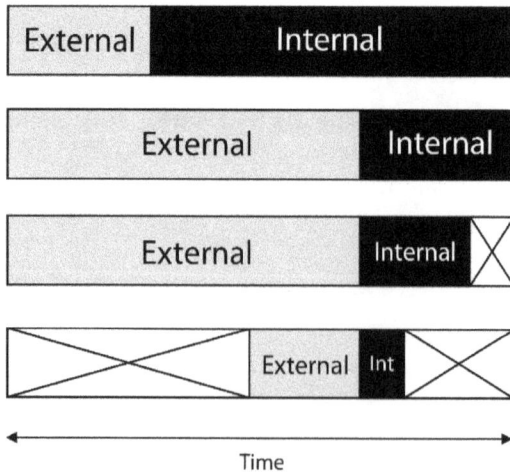

The transformation process consists of four steps:

1. Identify and separate internal and external set-up
2. Convert internal to external
3. Decrease internal set-up, and
4. Combine and eliminate tasks to decrease internal and external set-up.

Remarkably, the machine change-over model also describes what happens in kaizen with respect to people's knowledge and learning, as well as the concerns that workers have about the changes that are underway.

It also describes what leaders must do with respect to their beliefs and assumptions about people, management, and other critical knowledge in the change-over from conventional leadership to Lean leadership [6].

The process to change-over an executive's mindset from batch-and-queue thinking to flow is also a four-step process:

1. Recognize internal (tacit) conventional management beliefs and assumptions.
2. Convert internal (tacit) conventional management beliefs and assumptions to external (explicit).
3. Reduce internal (tacit) conventional management beliefs and assumptions.
4. Decrease internal (tacit) and external (explicit) conventional management beliefs and assumptions.

It turns out that a Lean transformation is a fractal (repeating pattern from small to large scale) change-over problem.

It is a simple and practical model that accurately describes change on three levels: kaizen, personal (leader), and organizational.

Improved LEI Model

The Lean Enterprise Institute and the Lean Enterprise Academy recently created a Lean transformation model [3] that is quite good because it accurately represents of how Toyota developed and evolved the Toyota Production System and The Toyota Way.

The LEI model, like anything, can be improved. Specifically, by including a greater level of detail to make it more specific and actionable. The added details are consistent with the history and evolution of Toyota's management thinking and practice.

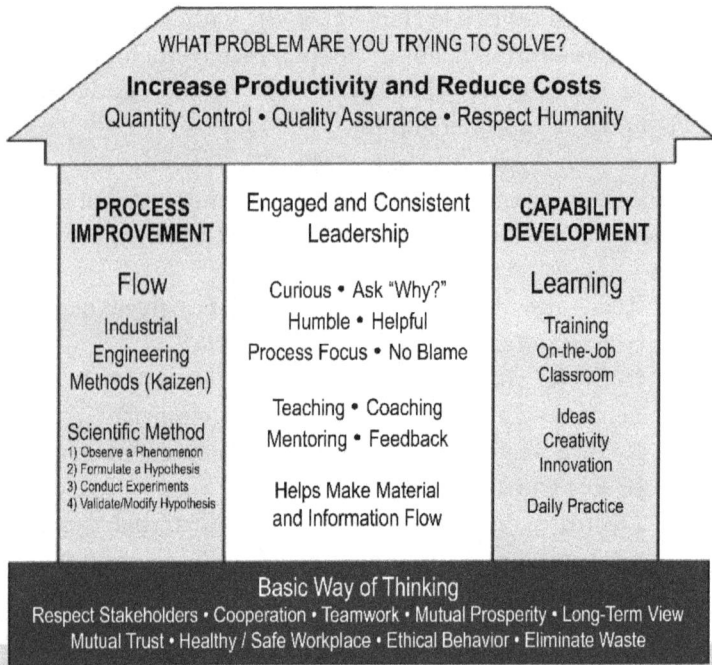

The "Basic Way of Thinking" is the foundation for success. Most business leaders lack this "Basic Way of Thinking," and, as a result, are unable to emulate Toyota in even the simplest ways. Their transformation efforts fall far short of expectations and usually do harm to people.

3P Model

Production preparation process (3P) is a method developed by sensei Chihiro Nakao [7] to build quality into a process for producing a product or service. The 3P process creates a method for production that satisfies the requirements for "product design quality, required production volume, target cost, target date" [8].

The 3P process helps an organization avoid expensive and time-consuming re-work caused by a lack of consideration to the many important details associated with the introduction of new items to production. The idea is to begin a new process with zero large problems, a minimum of problems, and then rapidly correct small problems as they arise.

The image below compares the characteristics of conventional batch-and-queue production based on economies of scale (middle column) to the usual way of Lean transformation.

Design Element	Characteristics	Usual Way of Lean Transformation
1. Machines / Equipment	Large, Complex, Expensive, Multi-Functional	Sophisticated Leadership at Highest Levels (e.g. MBA Mindset / Opinion Method)
2. Tooling	Complex, Expensive, Single Application	Complex Expensive Classroom Training and Change Management Programs
3. Layout / Flow	Large Footprint, Batch Processing, Slow Checks, Long Queue Time	Complex Process, Reviews, Approvals (Bureaucracy)

Unfortunately, extensive empirical evidence collected over decades tell us that the usual way of Lean transformation invariably leads to Fake Lean or failure. So we must consider a new way.

The image below compares the characteristics of flow production (middle column) based on the 3P way of Lean transformation. Closely study the differences between the two images.

Design Element	Characteristics	3P Way of Lean Transformation
1. Process / Flow	Small Footprint, One-Piece Processing, Quick Check, No Queue Time	Kaizen (Ideas & Trystorming), PDSA
2. Tooling	Simple, Inexpensive, Multi-Application	Mostly OJT, Simple Inexpensive Visual Controls
3. Machines / Equipment	Small, Simple, Inexpensive, Single Function	Basic Leadership at All Levels (Engineering Mindset / Scientific Method)

Give the above method a try. If it does not work as anticipated (gap), then apply the PDSA cycle shown on the following page (right-side path) to improve the process. And keep improving the process again and again thereafter.

Questions to consider:

- Which of the three models presented seems easiest to grasp and which seems more difficult to grasp?
- Is the model that is easiest to grasp a better model than the one that is harder to grasp?
- The Deming (PDSA) cycle shown on the following page is activated by gaps between planned and actual. As *Critique of Lean* has shown, there have been many gaps between plan and actual in the effort to advance Lean over the last 30 years. Why is it that strident advocates of PDSA have not practiced it?
- How should the PDSA cycle have been applied to the advancement of Lean over the last 30 years?

- What problems should the PDSA cycle have been applied to in the advancement of Lean over the last 30 years?

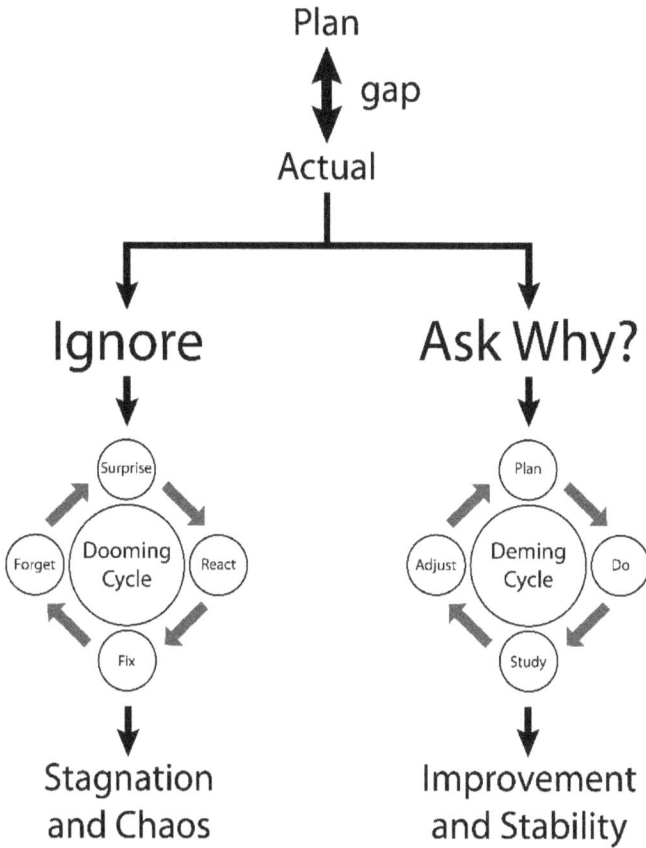

Plan

↕ gap

Actual

Ignore

Surprise
Forget — Dooming Cycle — React
Fix

Stagnation and Chaos

Ask Why?

Plan
Adjust — Deming Cycle — Do
Study

Improvement and Stability

People Love Craft

Time has proven that people seem to have an almost instinctive negative reaction to management innovations that affect their work, especially anything that might result in higher output. Why do workers have this negative reaction? Why is it so durable across generations of workers? Where does it come from?

For many years, it seemed that the negative reaction to Lean came from what people heard, read about, or experienced. This, in turn, generated the same six criticisms of progressive management since the beginning of Scientific Management in the late 1800s through Lean management today. Workers fear that progressive management will harm them by:

- De-humanizing them
- Speeding them up and burning them out
- De-skilling them
- Making them less knowledgeable about the work
- Making them less creative, more robotic
- And, worst of all, making them unemployed

A close reading of early books critical of industrialization and the early forms of progressive management reveal a different origin, one that is deeply encoded in the human brain. The critics focused on many aspects, but gave special attention to division of labor, the drift away from craft production, and the growing use of standardization and complex machinery in modern industrial production. It seems that removing craft from work, de-skilling workers, is a more significant concern that anyone truly realizes.

Craft production represented much more than just craft. It represented work as an integral part of humanity: life, relationships, bonds to the local community, ingenuity, a sense of worth, fulfillment, the continuance of life, and so on. And, the writings of the late 1800s and early 1900s included reference to virtues common among all religions such as humanity, honesty, justice, sacrifice, effort, and altruism. Standardization, in particular, turned noble craft work into something vulgar because of its sameness in work and in product and, especially, because of the loss of humanity in something so fundamental to life as work.

Think about this: For all of human history, craft production was the way things were made and spawned simple principles and mechanisms for honest trade among people in a community. Then, in only the last 250 years, machines and industries were developed to facilitate production and new methods for conducting business transactions were created, both of which became more sophisticated over time. This fundamentally and greatly changed the nature of work that humans had experienced for tens of thousands of years.

What humans had long known – small scale output, small batch processing, simple tools, simple machines, all employed for the purpose of survival or, later, earning a living – was disappearing. The link between the producer, an individual, and the consumer, another individual, was changing.

The post-Civil War period saw industry grow and business methods change, from doing work simply to earn a living to profiting from investment in goods (trade) and industrial production, and the development of strategies (often dishonest) to gain advantage by one business over another business. Work that in the past was done by one person from start to finish, was now done by a "concatenation of industrial processes" [9] focused on profit-minded ends.

The scope and scale of business grew and led to more complicated business strategies to obtain scale and monopoly power through consolidation. Batch-and-queue processing grew   ever-larger in scale, and then along came progressive Scientific Management in the early 1900s, whose purpose was to increase the productive output of companies and entire industries to satisfy the demands of a growing population, and whose intent was to do good things for the country and improve the lives of workers.

The demands on workers steadily increased and were more closely scrutinized by management. The notion of machine efficiency transferred to a new idea of human efficiency thanks to Scientific Management, where the stopwatch was first introduced. Work became more closely regulated and workers came under closer surveillance than ever before, in part to achieve greater financial gains for the owner. (Note that while Scientific Management sought to secure greater financial gains for workers as well, that often was not he outcome due to the greed of owners and managers). Workers became a small cog in a large machine of someone else's design and for someone else's benefit.

As money became the controlling factor in management decision-making, differential interests quickly emerged. Much in the same way there was a division in labor, there became a division in interests from historical norms. The interests of business and industry ("pecuniary interests," i.e. money-making) increasingly diverged from the interests of individual workers and the community.

The profit motive of business induces a condition in leaders that I call "socio-economic dissociation," wherein money (costs and profits) takes on a far greater importance than people, especially workers. Of course, business leaders were not all the same in how they viewed people and money. Then, as today, there is a spectrum of socio-economic dissociation. Generally, however, business leaders' strategies sought to put competitors at a disadvantage, and so the same thinking would soon apply to workers: Labor became capital's competitor. And capital was, in the long run, destined to win because the deck was stacked against workers as a result of the influential classical economic principles that owners hewed to.

This, in turn, led to a chronic state of derangement among business leaders that impaired the relationship between labor and capital and resulted in exploitation of workers. Personal relationships and other important values long associated with work, were disrupted. No longer would the individual producer, the craftsman, have a relationship with the individual who buys and uses the product (or service). Direct interaction with paying customers ceased.

Improvements in business processes, mechanical and otherwise, promoted greater interest in profits and less interest on the how modern management practices affected workers. Owners were largely untroubled by negative human impact until forced to recon with it as labor unions arose.

Division of labor, standardization, large scale batch-and-queue processes, and mechanization offered nothing in the way of restoring humanity to work, other than work rules negotiated in worker's behalf by labor unions, because management continued to suffer from socio-economic dissociation as the profit motive remained the controlling interest. Then, along comes the idea of flow in the early 1900s. It too offers little in the way of restoring humanity to work operating under the rule of "division of labor" – that is until Toyota Motor Corporation comes along.

The Craft of Kaizen

Toyota engineers, with input from other sources, developed a new process through trial-and-error that helps with the goal of achieving flow while simultaneously, and to an acceptable degree, helps restore humanity to work – especially if the new process is practiced on a daily basis. That process is kaizen. It is craft work that respects workers and other stakeholders, and importantly, is required if one wishes to achieve and improve flow. So, kaizen is sympathetic to both the daily needs of workers and the needs of business owners, as the enterprise struggles to satisfy customers' ever-changing wants and needs. This is why kaizen – Toyota's industrial engineering-based kaizen – is so important.

Yet, kaizen alone cannot engage human affection for craft work and connectivity to other humans that is deeply encoded in the human brain. Something more is needed, which must be supplied by top managers, but often missing. That is, leaders who are free of dissociative intellectual complex. If dissociative intellectual complex is present, workers will be deeply and forever suspicious of management, and may even think that their desire to improve productivity is a conspiracy to de-humanize workers, speed them up and burn them out, de-skill them, take away their knowledge, take away their creativity, and, ultimately, cost them their job. This outcome is a *fait accompli* when top managers adopt Lean management while the profit motive remains their controlling interest. The commonplace nature of Fake Lean is workers' worst nightmare come true.

However, not all managers are afflicted by socio-economic dissociation, and this is what workers need from management and which must accompany Toyota kaizen. Some business leaders see profit as a consequence of work done well, which means that people, especially employees, come before profits. This of course, does not negate the importance of profits.

What it actually does is establish the correct priority and relationship so that the business can continuously adapt and improve in response to changing times made possible by workers who are engaged in their work as a craft, thereby resulting in profits when times are good and when times are bad. Workers can go about their daily craft work with human contact in an industrial system of divided labor and standardization that is enmeshed with a great variety of modern mechanical and electronic machines.

We admire the company Toyota, but what that really means is that we admire the people of Toyota and those who contributed to the creation of its management system of which kaizen, craft work, is integral. Unfortunately, that is not the case for Lean.

Taiichi Ohno and his colleagues solved an immensely important problem, not perfectly, but in a way that is responsive to the fundamental nature of humans and their relationship with work and with each other.

Questions to consider:

- Why did the producers who gave us Lean largely ignore Toyota's industrial engineering-based kaizen methods in the initial presentation of Lean to business leaders?
- Why did the producers who gave us Lean largely ignore Toyota's industrial engineering-based kaizen methods in later decades as they worked to advance Lean?
- By largely ignoring Toyota's industrial engineering-based kaizen methods, Lean has become known as a method for process improving without kaizen. What is Lean without kaizen?
- What can be done to gain interest in Toyota's industrial engineering-based kaizen methods among thousands of companies, large and small, that have adopted Lean and whose leaders think kaizen is not needed because that is what they have been told (or surmise).
- The absence of kaizen as a core method in Lean has led to absence of kaizen in businesses that have adopted Lean, which reinforces managers' historical perceptions of workers as merely "direct labor." How can this perception, and its corollary, the substitution of

- technology for labor, be reversed so that the value of kaizen can emerge?

- The recent revival of the craft movement in micro- and small-scale production reflects a fundamental dissatisfaction with divided labor and standardization found in big business. In what other ways can industrial workers be given more opportunities to perform craft work?

- How can leadership and management be converted from task work to craft work so that it is performed every day with far fewer errors and much greater skill?

Comparison of LEI and Shingijutsu USA Action Plans

Lean Enterprise Institute "Lean Action Plan"[1]	Shingijutsu USA Action Plan[2]
Step 1 - Getting Started	**Step 1 – Commitment to Kaizen**
• **Find a change agent**, a leader who will take personal responsibility for the lean transformation.	• Management recognizes the need for significant change and is willing to change everything. Top leader is the change owner and is fully committed.
• **Get the lean knowledge**, via a sensei or consultant, who can teach lean techniques and how to implement them as part of a system, not as isolated programs.	• Learn kaizen from experienced teachers.
• Find a lever by **seizing a crisis** or by creating one to begin the transformation. If your company currently isn't in crisis, focus attention on a lean competitor or find a lean customer or supplier who will make demands for dramatically better performance.	• Crisis already exists, whether visible or not.
• **Forget grand strategy** for the moment.	• Be world class in all processes.
• **Map the value streams**, beginning with the current state of how material and information flow now, then drawing a leaner future state of how they should flow and creating an implementation plan with timetable.	• Not necessary to map value streams.
• **Begin as soon as possible** with an important and visible activity.	• Create a kaizen promotion office.
• **Demand immediate results**.	• Form kaizen teams and begin kaizen simultaneously in shop and office.
• As soon as you've got momentum, **expand your scope** to link improvements in the value streams and move beyond the shop floor to office processes.	• N/A
Step 2 - Creating an Organization to Channel Your Value Streams	**Step 2 – Continuously Improve Without Doing Harm to People**
• Reorganize your firm by product family and value stream.	• Reorganize work by product family.
• Create a lean promotion function.	• Completed in Step 1.
• Deal with excess people at the outset, and then promise that no one will lose their job in the future due to the introduction of lean techniques.	• Do not lay people off as a result of kaizen. Use kaizen make good people and good product. Allow employees to think and be creative and innovative.
• Devise a growth strategy.	• Strive for stable long-term growth.
• Remove the anchor-draggers.	• Ensure participation in kaizen is broad based, managers and workers, supporters and doubters.
• Once you've fixed something, fix it again.	• Kaizen never ends.
• "Two steps forward and one step backward is O.K.; no steps forward is not O.K."	• N/A
Step 3 - Install Business Systems to Encourage Lean Thinking	**Step 3 – Eliminate This Step (Step 4 Becomes Step 3)**
• Utilize policy deployment.	• Begin using policy deployment (move to Step 2).
• Create a lean accounting system.	• Transition to Lean accounting (move to Step 2).
• Pay your people in relation to the performance of your firm.	• Create a profit-sharing program (move to Step 1).
• Make performance measures transparent.	• Eliminate non-Lean performance measures (move to Steps 1 and 2).
• Teach lean thinking and skills to everyone.	• Teach structured problem-solving during kaizen (move to Step 1).
• Right-size your tools, such as production equipment and information systems.	• Right-size machines, tools, etc. (move to Step 1).
Step 4 - Completing the Transformation	**Step 4 – Kaizen Forever**
• Convince your suppliers and customers to take the steps just described.	• Work with suppliers and customers to improve processes that affect one another.
• Develop a lean global strategy.	• Promote people based on kaizen capabilities and interpersonal skills.
• Convert from top-down leadership to leadership based on questioning, coaching, and teaching and rooted in the scientific method of plan-do-check-act.	• Managers teach subordinates what they have learned in kaizen (move to Step 1).

1 "Lean Action Plan," http://www.lean.org/WhatsLean/GettingStarted.cfm, accessed 15 March 2017
2 Based on personal Emiliani's experience implementing TPS+TW with Shingijutsu USA

6

Closing Comments

Summary of Criticisms

In his opening keynote at the LEIs Lean Transformation Summit 2017 in Carlsbad, California, James P. Womack said [1]:

> "I underestimated the entrenchment of traditional
> and modern management thinking."

Indeed. This is the result of a near-singular focus on *action* and a near-total ignorance of *reaction*. By action, I mean focusing on the creation and evolution of TPS at Toyota and the creation and advancement of its derivative, Lean. By reaction, I mean unawareness or unwillingness to acknowledge how business leaders react to progressive management. Business leaders' negative reaction to progressive management has been clearly and comprehensively documented throughout history, from Scientific Management to TPS and to Lean. Workers' negative reaction has also been clearly documented throughout history.

This glaring underestimation of the entrenchment of management thinking has been consequential to the lives and livelihood of workers world-wide. How could the 30-plus year work of a social scientist largely overlook how humans respond to progressive management [2]? As one of the originators of Lean and its most vigorous promoter, Womack's apparent bias against negative reactions and the failure to quickly identify and implement countermeasures have been to the detriment of Lean and its users.

So, nearly 30 years after the start of the Lean movement, there is widespread understanding that things have not gone according to plan [3]: e.g. Fake Lean organizations far exceed Real Lean organizations, bureaucracy and new overhead functions were created that enabled managers to delegate Lean, and there are too many definitions of Lean which has resulted great confusion, etc. Of course, there have been some notable examples of Lean transformation success – particularly those organizations that worked with former Toyota sensei [4, 5] – yet they are far fewer in number than anyone expected.

The Ohnoist critique of Lean presented in this volume identified the sources and factors that led to the shortfall. The main criticisms of Lean are summarized as follows:

- Overconfidence on the part of the Lean producers to think they could easily understand Toyota's thinking, and hence lead others, without ever actually creating, with their own hands, a functioning flowline in an industrial setting. That they would become the arbiters of Lean thought and practice is remarkable. The unwillingness of people to challenge them made matters worse.

- Promoting corporate wealth creation instead of humbler, more basic, aspirations and outcomes; the kind of positive results that everyone wants to experience, such as process simplification (for both workers' and managers' processes), made possible by human creativity and innovative ideas in a fun and non-threatening work environment.

- Judging the history of Scientific Management to be irrelevant, and therefore useless to learn from to address current-day problems regarding the acceptance and advancement of progressive Lean management.

- Not understanding the strength to which people are attracted to tools to improve existing management practices, and, conversely, the near-total lack of interest in a completely new system of management.

- Waiting 20 years to transition from Lean production to Lean management.

- Waiting 20 years to focus on Lean leadership.

- Waiting until 2008 to explicitly recognize, and until 2014 to aggressively promote, "Respect for People." The many layoffs that came as a result of Lean are a tragedy and its most obvious and regrettable failure.

- Not emphasizing Toyota's industrial engineering-based kaizen methods, strongly, from the very start.

- Not understanding the critical importance of kaizen for teaching people "Continuous Improvement," "Respect for People," and the relationship between the two.

- Not emphasizing flow, and the inseparable connection between it, kaizen, and "Respect for People."

- Underestimating the strength of classical and neoclassical economics in shaping management thinking and decision-making and ensuring commitment to conventional management practice despite the existence of more advanced methods.

- Vastly overestimating the extent to which conservative-minded business leaders might be interested in a new progressive system of management, the extent of their curiosity, and the extent of their interest in improving their leadership behaviors and competencies.

- Overestimating the extent to which business leaders care about people. If Lean is, as often said, "all about people," then it is clear that most leaders don't care about people, particularly when the distance between them and the shop or office floor, both physically or in rank, is great.

- Not understanding importance of craft production in human evolution and why the need for craft production in some form (kaizen) remains a necessity for human existence, both personally and professionally.

It is apparent that the Lean producers did the Plan-Do (action), but it struggled greatly with the Study-Adjust (reaction) part of the Deming cycle. The lack of timely problem recognition and corrective action stands out as a major recurring error that compounded the negative human impact of these miscalculations.

As a result, there continues to exist deeply-rooted negative associations of Lean to layoffs, Taylorism, bureaucratic ("check-the-box") Lean, and improvement without achieving much in the way of actual business results (highest quality, lowest cost, shortest lead-time, etc.).

Given these continuing problems, one would expect Lean to have limited appeal going forward. However, it seems that Lean continues to thrive, at least for now. Branding, marketing, the illusion of equivalence with Toyota, etc., have always been strong and must continue for Lean to survive. However, these tactics discourage people from engaging in careful research, for they would no doubt discover the same things as have been presented in this volume [2].

But, much to the dismay of teachers everywhere, students taught how to do research in school rarely do research once they become employed. Despite the consequential nature of progressive management on people's lives and livelihoods, information handed to them is assumed to be both accurate and useful [2]. Coupled with an absence of critical thinking (also to the dismay of teachers everywhere), the result is for former students to labor under illusions and to lament, years later, how things did not work out as they anticipated.

This is the peril of outsourcing one's thinking. People believe they understand things that do not [2]. Over time, a collective knowledge about Lean has grown to a proportion such that there is virtually no interest in searching for the truth. To do so means going backwards in time when almost everyone wants to (or is told to) go forward. It is simpler and requires less energy and thought to accept what one is told by authority figures with impeccable credentials coupled with extensive advertising and promotion. The collective confidence in understanding Lean reinforces each individual's sense of understanding Lean. This is yet another illusion.

The strength of the Lean community – a shared belief in Lean and a shared understanding of Lean – is also its weakness, as few possess the detailed knowledge required to either advance it or defend it. They must, therefore, rely on others such as Womack and Jones for detailed knowledge. But, that responsibility goes unfulfilled when movement leaders are misinformed and unresponsive due to overconfidence in their understanding of TPS and The Toyota Way.

The nature of Lean management (and TPS and Scientific Management before that) as a new system of management poses an enormous challenge to those who seek to advance it. Progressive management is at odds in nearly every way with the traditional manager's mindset (see page 142). In *Efficiency and Uplift: Scientific Management and the Progressive Era 1890-1920* [6], Professor Samuel Haber said the following:

> "The very notion of a completely integrated, scientific system for the factory was a distraction [to businessmen]. The truly 'scientific' standard for 'an honest day's work'… could not be established and maintained unless the entire factory was systematized. Yet most business firms, as Taylor himself once noted, need only be more efficient than their competitors. This was one of the reasons that businessmen preferred efficiency stunts, devices, and

mechanisms to a complete system of scientific management. The adoption of a complete system was often not the most profitable use of investment capital. Here... commercial efficiency did not automatically come first. The system should be adopted, Taylor's most orthodox disciples asserted, even when it might not be a paying investment."

Decades of empirical evidence indicates that the same mindset exists among managers when it comes to both TPS and Lean. Business leaders have a powerful preference for only limited adjustments to their existing management practice [7]. This undercuts the common argument that business leaders don't practice Lean because Lean, itself, is difficult. Instead, the difficulty is in challenging the underlying economic, social, political, and historical preconceptions that inform the managerial mindset and decision-making [8].

Questions to consider:

- This Ohnoist critique of Lean identified time as a significant feature in recognizing and correcting problems related to the understanding and advancement of Lean. What is the relationship between Toyota's industrial engineering-based kaizen method, consistently diminished in the Lean orthodoxy, and time?

- How can the collective confidence in the understanding of Lean be transformed to a collective doubt in understanding Lean in order to recognize problems faster and make effective improvements (see chart on next page)?

- TPS demands a different economics, while Lean (pre-2008, before "Respect for People") did not. What additional countermeasures can be applied to correct this error?

- How will the Lean community respond to the obvious truth that the vast majority of business leaders prefer to build on what they know and existing methods and systems versus replace what they know and build anew?
- How will the Lean community respond to the apparent truth that the vast majority of business leaders prioritize profits over efficiency?
- What are some ways in which the underlying economic, social, political, and historical preconceptions possessed by business leaders can be challenged in order for Lean to transition from a niche management practice to a common (widespread) management practice?
- Great hope remains that business leaders will adopt Lean management. What if the competitive marketplace for management methods does the opposite and de-selects Lean because it does not further the interests of capital? What, then, is the Lean strategy?

Comparison of Toyota Production System and Lean

Method	Toyota Production System	Lean (1988)	Lean (1996→)
Designer	Industrial Engineers	Mechanical Engineer*	Social Scientists**
Goal	Cost Reduction Productivity Improvement	Quality Productivity	Maximize Customer Value
Principles	Continuous Improvement Respect for People	Continuous Improvement	Specify Value Identify the Value Stream Flow Pull Perfection
Normal Condition	Flow	Flow	Perfect Processes
Focus of Improvement	Human	Technical	Technical
Primary Teaching Method	Genba Kaizen	Team Leader	Classroom
Object of Interest	Waste, Unevenness, Unreasonableness	Inventories	Value Creating Activities
Desired Outcome	Customer Satisfaction Survival	High Plant Performance	Perfect Value

*   John Krafcik, "Triumph of the Lean Production System" (1988) https://www.lean.org/downloads/MITSloan.pdf
** James P. Womack and Daniel T. Jones, Lean Thinking (1996) and http://www.lean.org/WhatsLean/ (accessed 15 March 2017)

How the Lean Producers Have Described Lean

Description	Year
Toyota Production System	1988
Continuous Improvement	1990
Wealth Creation	1996
A Management System	2007
A Learning System	2010
TPS + The Toyota Way	2014
A Strategy	2016
TBD	?

How Toyota Describes TPS and The Toyota Way

Toyota Production System is "a way of making things"

The Toyota Way "…clarifies the values and business methods that all employees should embrace in order to carry out the Guiding Principles at Toyota…"

Progressive Management Has Always Been

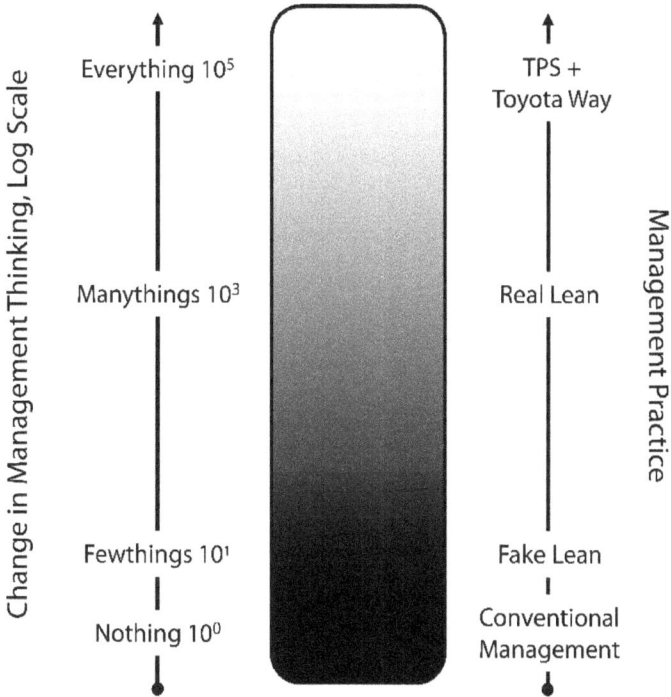

Change in Management Thinking, Log Scale

Management Practice

Everything 10^5

TPS +
Toyota Way

Manythings 10^3

Real Lean

Fewthings 10^1

Fake Lean

Nothing 10^0

Conventional
Management

A Huge Challenge for Managers

Appendix

Professor Emiliani's
Qualifications for Critiquing Lean

Training
Kaizen training by Shingijutsu Co. Ltd. (1994-1997) and
Shingijutsu USA (2014-2017 with sensei Chihiro Nakao).

Experience
23 years of kaizen practice in manufacturing, supply chain
management, and higher education (academic and
administrative work).

Peer-Reviewed Journal Papers
1. "Evolution in Lean Teaching," submitted for publication,
   October 2016
2. "Engaging Faculty in Lean Teaching," *International Journal of
   Lean Six Sigma*, Vol. 6, Issue 1, 2015
3. "Henry Gantt: Lean Before There Was Lean," *Lean
   Management Journal*, Volume 4, Issue 7, September 2014, pp.
   12-13.
4. "Music as a Framework to Better Understand Lean
   Leadership," *Leadership and Organizational Development Journal*,
   Vol. 34, Issue 5, 2013, pp. 407-426.
5. "Lean Management Failure at HMRC," *Management Services*,
   Journal of the Institute of Management Services, Vol. 55,
   No. 4, Winter 2011, pp. 13-15. **Invited paper.**
6. "The History of Flow," with P. Seymour and P. Found,
   Lean Management Journal, September-October 2011, pp. 28-
   31.
7. "Frank George Woollard: Forgotten Pioneer of Flow
   Production," with P.J. Seymour, *Journal of Management
   History*, Volume 17, Issue 1, 2011, pp. 66-87.
8. "Historical Lessons in Purchasing and Supplier
   Relationship Management," *Journal of Management History*,
   Vol. 16, No. 1, 2010, pp. 116-136.

9. "Standardized Work for Executive Leadership," *Leadership and Organizational Development Journal*, Vol. 29, No. 1, 2008, pp. 24-46.

10. "Improving Management Education," *Quality Assurance in Education*, Vol. 14, No. 4, 2006, pp. 363-384.

11. "Origins of Lean Management in America: The Role of Connecticut Businesses," *Journal of Management History*, Vol. 12, No. 2, 2006, pp. 167-184.

12. "Leaders Lost in Transformation," with D.J. Stec, *Leadership and Organizational Development Journal*, Vol. 26, No. 5, 2005, pp. 370-387.

13. "Using Kaizen to Improve Graduate Business School Degree Programs," *Quality Assurance in Education*, Vol. 13, No. 1, 2005, pp. 37-52. **Highly Commended Paper Award** from Emerald Publishing.

14. "Unintended Responses to a Traditional Purchasing Performance Metric," with D.J. Stec and L.P. Grasso, *Supply Chain Management: An International Journal*, Vol. 10, No. 3, 2005, pp. 150-156.

15. "Using Value Stream Maps to Improve Leadership," with D.J. Stec, *Leadership and Organizational Development Journal*, Vol. 25, No. 8, 2004, pp. 622-645.

16. "Improving Business School Courses by Applying Lean Principles and Practices," *Quality Assurance in Education*, Vol. 12, No. 4, 2004, pp. 175-187.

17. "Is Management Education Beneficial to Society?," *Management Decision*, Vol. 42, No. 3/4, 2004, pp. 481-498.

18. "Linking Leaders' Beliefs to Their Behaviors and Competencies," *Management Decision*, Vol. 41, No. 9, 2003, pp. 893-910.

19. "A Mathematical Logic Approach to the Shareholder vs. Stakeholder Debate," *Management Decision*, Vol. 39, No. 8, 2001, pp. 618-622.

20. "Redefining the Focus of Investment Analysts," *The TQM Journal*, Vol. 13, No. 1, 2001, pp. 34-50. **Citation of Excellence Award** from *Emerald Management Reviews*.

170   Critique of Lean

21. "The False Promise of 'What Gets Measured Gets Managed'," *Management Decision*, Vol. 38, No. 9, 2000, pp. 612-615.
22. "Supporting Small Businesses in their Transition to Lean Production," *Supply Chain Management: An International Journal*, Vol. 5, No. 2, 2000, pp. 66-70.
23. "The Oath of Management," *Management Decision*, Vol. 38, No. 4, 2000, pp. 261-262.
24. "Cracking the Code of Business," *Management Decision*, Vol. 38, No. 2, 2000, pp. 60-79. **Highly Commended Paper Award** from Emerald Publishing.
25. "The Making of a Lean Aerospace Supply Chain," *Supply Chain Management: An International Journal*, Vol. 4, No. 3, 1999, pp. 135-144.
26. "Lean Behaviors," *Management Decision*, Vol. 36, No. 9, 1998, pp. 615-631. **Outstanding Paper Award,** 1998 volume of *Management Decision*.
27. "Continuous Personal Improvement," *Journal of Workplace Learning*, Vol. 10, No. 1, 1998, pp. 29-38.

Books
1. *Speed Leadership: A Better Way To Lead In Rapidly Changing Times*, Second Edition, ISBN 978-0-9898631-6-2, October 2015
2. *Shingijutsu-Kaizen: The Art of Discovery and Learning*, with R. Wood and M. Herscher, ISBN-13: 978-0-9898631-5-5, October 2015
3. *Lean Is Not Mean: 68 Practical Lessons in Lean Leadership*, ISBN 978-0-9898631-3-1, June 2015
4. *Lean University: A Guide to Renewal and Prosperity*, ISBN 978-0-9898631-2-4, June 2015
5. *Lean Teaching: A Guide to Becoming a Better Teacher*, ISBN 978-0-9898631-1-7, June 2015
6. *Kaizen Forever: Teachings of Chihiro Nakao*, with K. Yoshino and R. Go, ISBN 978-0-9898631-0-0, May 2015
7. *Moving Forward Faster: The Mental Evolution from Fake Lean to REAL Lean*, ISBN 978-0-9845400-1-3, January 2011
8. *REAL LEAN: Unsolved Problems in Lean Management*, Volume Six, ISBN 978-0-9845400-0-6, October 2010

9. *REAL LEAN: Strategies for Lean Management Success*, Volume Five, ISBN 978-0-9722591-9-4, January 2010
10. F.G. Woollard, *Principles of Mass and Flow Production*, Special 55th Anniversary Reprint Edition, with Bob Emiliani, ISBN 978-0-9722591-8-7, January 2009
11. *REAL LEAN: Learning the Craft of Lean Management*, Volume Four, ISBN 978-0-9722591-7-0, October 2008
12. *REAL LEAN: The Keys to Sustaining Lean Management*, Volume Three, ISBN 978-0-9722591-6-3, May 2008
13. *Practical Lean Leadership: A Strategic Leadership Guide for Executives*, ISBN 978-0-9722591-5-6, January 2008
14. *REAL LEAN: Critical Issues and Opportunities in Lean Management*, Volume Two, ISBN 978-0-9722591-4-9, July 2007
15. *Better Thinking, Better Results: Case Study and Analysis of an Enterprise-Wide Lean Transformation*, with D. Stec, L. Grasso, and J. Stodder, second edition, ISBN 978-0-9722591-2-5, March 2007
16. *REAL LEAN: Understanding the Lean Management System*, Volume One, ISBN 978-0-9722591-1-8, January 2007
17. *Better Thinking, Better Results: Using the Power of Lean as Total Business Solution*, with D. Stec, L. Grasso, and J. Stodder, first edition, ISBN 0-9722591-0-4, January 2003 (out of print)

Book Chapter

"Ohno's Insights on Human Nature" in *Taiichi Ohno's Workplace Management: Special 100th Birthday Edition*, T. Ohno, translated by J. Miller, McGraw-Hill, New York, NY, 2012, pp. 157-162

End Notes

All URLs accessed on 15 March 2017

Preface
[1] Krafcik, J.F. (1988), "Triumph of the Lean Production System," *Sloan Management Review*, Vol. 30, No. 1, pp. 41-52

[2] Womack, J., Jones, D., and Roos, D. (1990), *The Machine that Changed the World*, Rawson Associates, New York, NY

[3] Planet Lean, http://planet-lean.com

[4] Womack, J. and Jones, D. (1996), *Lean Thinking*, Simon & Schuster, New York, NY

[5] "The word 'critic' comes from Greek κριτικός (kritikós), meaning 'able to discern,' which is a Greek derivation of the word κριτής (krités), meaning a person who offers reasoned judgment or analysis, value judgment, interpretation or observation." https://en.wikipedia.org/wiki/Critic

[6] Ohno, T. (1988), *Toyota Production System: Beyond Large-Scale Production*, Productivity Press, Portland, OR

[7] Ohno, T. (1988b), *Workplace Management*, Productivity Press, Portland, OR

[8] Lean Enterprise Institute, https://www.lean.org

[9] Lean Enterprise Academy http://www.leanuk.org

[10] Emiliani, B. (2015), *Lean Is Not Mean: 68 Practical Lessons in Lean Leadership*, The CLBM, LLC, Wethersfield, Conn., pp. 5-21, http://www.bobemiliani.com/wp-content/uploads/2016/03/LNM_Lesson_1_-Mean-6-22a.pdf

[11] Writings by the author and others that have been critical of Lean evoke a strong negative response from its originators, their surrogates, affiliated promoters, Lean celebrities, power-users, experts, neophytes, and others. Hypersensitivity to criticism coupled with an inability to acknowledge criticism as a method of improvement suggests a collective narcissism. This is made visible by the constant need for personal and professional affirmation and the need to challenge or extinguish perceived threats to Lean or to one's self. This phenomenon is well documented in social media.

Introduction
[1] Krafcik, J.F. (1988), "Triumph of the Lean Production System," *Sloan Management Review*, Vol. 30, No. 1, pp. 41-52
[2] Womack, J., Jones, D., and Roos, D. (1990), *The Machine that Changed the World*, Rawson Associates, New York, NY
[3] Day, P. (2007), "'Mr Toyota' is shy about being No 1," BBC News, http://news.bbc.co.uk/2/hi/business/6237110.stm, 25 June
[4] Stewart, T. and Raman, A. (2007), "Lessons from Toyota's Long Drive," *Harvard Business Review*, July-August, p. 80
[5] Womack, J. and Jones, D. (1996), *Lean Thinking*, Simon & Schuster, New York, NY
[6] Anon., "A Brief History of Lean," Lean Enterprise Institute, https://www.lean.org/WhatsLean/History.cfm

1. Failure to Learn from the Past
[1] Monden, Y. (1983), *Toyota Production System: Practical Approach to Production Management*, Engineering and Management Press, Norcross, GA.
[2] Ibid., p. i
[3] Ibid., p. 2
[4] Womack, J. and Jones, D. (1996), *Lean Thinking*, Simon & Schuster, New York, NY
[5] Shingijutsu USA, Inc., http://www.shingijutsuusa.com
[6] Emiliani, M.L. (2006), "Origins of Lean Management in America: The Role of Connecticut Businesses," *Journal of Management History*, Vol. 12 Issue 2, pp.167-184
[7] Taylor, F. W. (1911), *The Principles of Scientific Management*, Harper and Brothers, New York, NY
[8] Taylor, F. W. (1947), *Scientific Management: Comprising Shop Management, Scientific Management, Testimony Before the Special House Committee*, H. S. Person, Ed., Harper and Row Publishers, New York, NY (Testimony originally published in 1912), p. 191
[9] Emiliani, B. (2015), *Lean Is Not Mean: 68 Practical Lessons in Lean Leadership*, The CLBM, LLC, Wethersfield, Conn., pp. 175-178, http://www.bobemiliani.com/wp-content/uploads/2016/07/LNM_Lesson_45_-Mean-6-22a.pdf

[10] Gantt, H. (1916), *Industrial Leadership*, Yale University Press, New Haven, Conn.

[11] Shinohara, I., (1988), *NPS: New Production System*, Productivity Press, Cambridge, MA, p. 155

[12] Toyota (2001), "The Toyota Way 2001," Toyota Motor Corporation, internal document, Toyota City (Nagoya), Japan, April

[13] Womack, J. (2007), "Respect for People," eLetter to the LEI community, 20 December, http://www.lean.org/womack/DisplayObject.cfm?o=755

2. Poor Interpretation of TPS

[1] Emiliani, B. *et al.*, (2007), *Better Thinking, Better Results: Case Study and Analysis of an Enterprise-Wide Lean Transformation*, second edition, The CLBM, LLC, Wethersfield, Conn.

[2] Toyota (2001), "The Toyota Way 2001," Toyota Motor Corporation, internal document, Toyota City (Nagoya), Japan, April

[3] Womack, J., Jones, D., and Roos, D. (1990), *The Machine that Changed the World*, Rawson Associates, New York, NY

[4] Womack, J. and Jones, D. (1996), *Lean Thinking*, Simon & Schuster, New York, NY

[5] Monden, Y. (1983), *Toyota Production System: Practical Approach to Production Management*, Engineering and Management Press, Norcross, GA.

[6] Krafcik, J.F. (1988), "Triumph of the Lean Production System," *Sloan Management Review*, Vol. 30, No. 1, pp. 41-52

[7] Sugimori, Y., Kusunoki, K., Cho, F. and Uchikawa, S. (1977), "Toyota Production System and Kanban System – Materialization of Just-in-Time and Respect-for-Human System," *International Journal of Production Research*, Vol. 15, No. 6, pp. 553-564 http://www.tandfonline.com/doi/abs/10.1080/00207547708943149

[8] Husar, M. (1991), "Corporate Culture: Toyota's Secret, Competitive Advantage," General Motors internal document, Ref. #70.2, 15 May. https://goo.gl/SsscVE

[9] Ohno, T. (1988), *Toyota Production System: Beyond Large-Scale Production*, Productivity Press, Portland, OR

[10] Ohno, T. (1988b), *Workplace Management*, Productivity Press, Portland, OR

[11] *Lean Lexicon* (2006), Lean Enterprise Institute, Cambridge, MA, 5th edition, pp. 60-62

[12] Womack, J. (2006), "Purpose, Process, People," 12 June, https://www.lean.org/womack/DisplayObject.cfm?o=742

[13] Jones, D. (2014), "What Lean Really Is," 11 September http://www.leanuk.org/article-pages/articles/2014/september/11/what-lean-really-is.aspx

[14] Ballé, M. and Jones D. (2014), "10 Signs You Respect Me As An Employee," *Fast Company*, 6 October https://www.fastcompany.com/3036623/the-future-of-work/10-signs-you-respect-me-as-an-employee

[15] Priolo, R. (2016), "Lean Thinking – The Making of a Book," 21 September, Planet Lean, http://planet-lean.com/writing-lean-thinking-the-authors-look-back

[16] Anon., (2016), "Lean Thinking at 20: A Q&A with Jim Womack and Dan Jones," Part 1, Lean Enterprise Institute, 28 September, https://www.lean.org/LeanPost/Posting.cfm?LeanPostId=635

[17] Anon., (2016), "Lean Thinking at 20: A Q&A with Jim Womack and Dan Jones," Part 2, Lean Enterprise Institute, 29 September, https://www.lean.org/LeanPost/Posting.cfm?LeanPostId=636

[18] Stacy Gleiss, (2016), "Lean Jesus: Church Efficacy and Efficiency," https://thesixfootbonsai.com/2016/06/26/lean-jesus-church-efficacy-and-efficiency/, 26 June

[19] Taylor, F.W. (1947), *Scientific Management: Comprising Shop Management, Principles of Scientific Management, Testimony Before the House Committee*, H. S. Person, Ed., Harper & Brothers Publishers, New York, NY, p. xii

[20] Woollard, F. G., and Emiliani, B. (2009), *Principles of Mass and Flow Production, 55th Anniversary Special Reprint Edition*, B. Emiliani, Ed., The CLBM, LLC. Wethersfield, Conn.
[21] Emiliani, M.L., (2013), "Music as a Framework to Better Understand Lean Leadership," *Leadership and Organizational Development Journal*, Vol. 34, Issue 5, pp. 407-426
[22] Taylor, F. W. (1911), *The Principles of Scientific Management*, Harper and Brothers, New York, NY, p. 131

3. Ignoring the Big Problems
[1] Planet Lean, http://planet-lean.com
[2] Lean Enterprise Institute, https://www.lean.org
[3] Lean Enterprise Academy http://www.leanuk.org
[4] Jones, D. (2014) "Planet-Lean.com interviews Daniel T. Jones and James P. Womack at the UK Lean Summit 2014," https://youtu.be/KYi6gkFYYpU, 23 December
[5] Emiliani, B. *et al.*, (2007), *Better Thinking, Better Results: Case Study and Analysis of an Enterprise-Wide Lean Transformation*, second edition, The CLBM, LLC, Wethersfield, Conn.
[6] Rother, M. (2016), "Scientific Thinking for Everyone," November, https://www.lean.org/coachingkata/Archive.cfm?KataItemId=53
[7] Ohno, T. (1988), *Toyota Production System: Beyond Large-Scale Production*, Productivity Press, Portland, OR, p. 59
[8] Ohno, T., with Mito, S., (1988), *Just-In-Time For Today and Tomorrow*, Productivity Press, Cambridge, MA, p. xii
[9] Shinohara, I., (1988), *NPS: New Production System*, Productivity Press, Cambridge, MA, p. 155
[10] Krafcik, J.F. (1988), "Triumph of the Lean Production System," *Sloan Management Review*, Vol. 30, No. 1, pp. 41-52
[11] Womack, J., Jones, D., and Roos, D. (1990), *The Machine that Changed the World*, Rawson Associates, New York, NY
[12] Womack, J. and Jones, D. (1996), *Lean Thinking*, Simon & Schuster, New York, NY
[13] Ruskin, J. (1862), *Unto This Last*, Penguin Classics, New York, NY, 1985

[14] Ingram, J. (1888), *A History of Political Economy*, MacMillan and Co., New York, NY

[15] Cook-Taylor, R.W., (1891), *The Modern Factory System*, Kegan Paul, Trench, Trübner & Co., Ltd., London, England

[16] Veblen, T. (1904), *The Theory of Business Enterprise*, Charles Scribner's Sons, New York, NY

4. Failure to Improve

[1] Ohno, T. (1988), *Toyota Production System: Beyond Large-Scale Production*, Productivity Press, Portland, OR, pp. 59-60

[2] Gilbreth, F. (1912), *Primer of Scientific Management*, D. Van Nostrand Company, New York, NY, pp. 14 and 68-69

[3] Woollard, F. G., and Emiliani, B. (2009), *Principles of Mass and Flow Production*, 55th *Anniversary Special Reprint Edition*, B. Emiliani, Ed., The CLBM, LLC. Wethersfield, Conn.

[4] Cooke, M. (1913), "The Spirit and Social Significance of Scientific Management," *Journal of Political Economy*, Vol. 21, No. 6, pp. 481-493

[5] Taylor, F. W. (1947), *Scientific Management: Comprising Shop Management, Scientific Management, Testimony Before the Special House Committee*, H. S. Person, Ed., Harper and Row Publishers, New York, NY (Testimony originally published in 1912).

[6] Taylor, F. W., (1895), "A Piece-Rate System," ASME *Transactions*, Vol. 16, pp. 856-903

[7] Taylor, F.W. (1903), "Shop Management," ASME *Transactions*, Vol. 24, pp. 1337-1480

[8] Taylor, F. W. (1911), *The Principles of Scientific Management*, Harper and Brothers, New York, NY

[9] Towne, H. (1886), "The Engineer as an Economist," ASME *Transactions*, Vol. 7, pp. 428-432

[10] Womack, J. (2016), "Dealing with Lean's Crazy Relatives," Planet Lean, 26 September, http://planet-lean.com/jim-womack-takes-on-the-legacy-of-taylor-and-ford

[11] Emiliani, B. (2011), *Moving Forward Faster: The Mental Evolution from Fake Lean to REAL Lean*, The CLBM, LLC, Wethersfield, Conn.

[12] Taylor, F. W. (1947), *Scientific Management: Comprising Shop Management, Scientific Management, Testimony Before the Special House Committee*, H. S. Person, Ed., Harper and Row Publishers, New York, NY (Testimony originally published in 1912), p. 191

[13] For a short biography of G. Charter Harrison, see https://en.wikipedia.org/wiki/G._Charter_Harrison

[14] For a short biography of Charles Bedaux, see https://en.wikipedia.org/wiki/Charles_Bedaux

[15] Krafcik, J.F. (1988), "Triumph of the Lean Production System," *Sloan Management Review*, Vol. 30, No. 1, pp. 41-52

[16] Shimokawa, K. and Fujimoto, T. Eds. (2009), *The Birth of Lean*, Lean Enterprise Institute, Cambridge, MA

[17] Womack, J.P., (2008), "The Toyota concept of 'respect for people," *Reliable Plant*, January, http://www.reliableplant.com/Read/9818

[18] Toyota (2001), "The Toyota Way 2001," Toyota Motor Corporation, internal document, Toyota City (Nagoya), Japan, April

[19] Anon., "Item 4. Human Resources Development: Compilation of the Toyota Way," http://www.toyota-global.com/company/history_of_toyota/75years/text/leaping_forward_as_a_global_corporation/chapter4/section7/item4.html

[20] Sugimori, Y., Kusunoki, K., Cho, F. and Uchikawa, S. (1977), "Toyota Production System and Kanban System – Materialization of Just-in-Time and Respect-for-Human System," *International Journal of Production Research*, Vol. 15, No. 6, pp. 558 http://www.tandfonline.com/doi/abs/10.1080/00207547708943149

[21] Monden, Y. (1983), *Toyota Production System: Practical Approach to Production Management*, Engineering and Management Press, Norcross, GA., p. 2

[22] Ohno, T. (1988), *Toyota Production System: Beyond Large-Scale Production*, Productivity Press, Portland, OR, p. xiii

[23] Cho, F. (2012), "Message from the Chairman of the Board," http://www.toyota-global.com/company/history_of_toyota/75years/message/index.html

[24] Anon., "The Lean Transformation Framework," Lean Enterprise Institute, https://www.lean.org/WhatsLean/TransformationFramework.cfm

5. What Next?

[1] Shinohara, I., (1988), *NPS: New Production System*, Productivity Press, Cambridge, MA, p. 155

[2] Emiliani, B. (2015), *Lean Is Not Mean: 68 Practical Lessons in Lean Leadership*, The CLBM, LLC, Wethersfield, Conn., pp. 5-21, http://www.bobemiliani.com/wp-content/uploads/2016/03/LNM_Lesson_1_-Mean-6-22a.pdf

[3] Anon., "The Lean Transformation Framework," Lean Enterprise Institute, https://www.lean.org/WhatsLean/TransformationFramework.cfm

[4] Emiliani, B. *et al.*, (2003), *Better Thinking, Better Results: Using the Power of Lean as Total Business Solution*, first edition, The CLBM, LLC, Wethersfield, Conn. pp. 248-254 (out of print)

[5] Shingo, S. (1985), *A Revolution in Manufacturing: The SMED System*, Productivity Press, Portland, OR, pp. 26-31

[6] Emiliani, B. (2011), *Moving Forward Faster: The Mental Evolution from Fake Lean to REAL Lean,* The CLBM, LLC, Wethersfield, Conn.

[7] Shingijutsu USA, Inc., http://www.shingijutsuusa.com

[8] Shingijutsu (2016), "Shingijutsu Super Genba Kaizen Workshop 3P," Training Workbook, April

[9] Veblen, T. (1904), *The Theory of Business Enterprise*, Charles Scribner's Sons, New York, NY, p. 276

6. Closing Comments

[1] Anderson, K. (2017), "Highlights and Reflections from the Lean Transformation Summit 2017," 14 March http://kbjanderson.com/highlights-and-reflections-from-the-lean-transformation-summit-2017/

[2] To understand why the Lean producers and others largely ignored the human response to progressive management, read Barrett, L. (2017), "The Secret History of Emotion," *The Chronicle of Higher Education*, 10 March, http://www.chronicle.com/article/The-Secret-History-of-Emotions/239357 Prof. Barret's search for the truth closely parallels my own search for the truth. History matters, and so do old books containing original source material. Poor interpretations distort to the truth and thus reduce the quality, reliability, and value of the work done by self and others.

[3] Jones, D. (2014), "Planet-Lean.com interviews Daniel T. Jones and James P. Womack at the UK Lean Summit 2014," https://youtu.be/KYi6gkFYYpU, 23 December

[4] Emiliani, B. *et al.*, (2007), *Better Thinking, Better Results: Case Study and Analysis of an Enterprise-Wide Lean Transformation*, second edition, The CLBM, LLC, Wethersfield, Conn.

[5] Kenney, C. (2011), *Transforming Health Care: Virginia Mason Medical Center's Pursuit of the Perfect Patient Experience*, CRC Press, Boca Raton, FL

[6] Haber, S. (1964), *Efficiency and Uplift: Scientific Management and the Progressive Era 1890-1920*, The University of Chicago Press, Chicago, Ill., pp. 16-17

[7] Smith, T. (2000), *Technology and Capital in the Age of Lean Production*, State University of New York Press, Albany, NY, Chapters 1-5

[8] Emiliani, B. (2011), *Moving Forward Faster: The Mental Evolution from Fake Lean to REAL Lean*, The CLBM, LLC, Wethersfield, Conn.

About the Author

About the Author

M.L. "Bob" Emiliani is a professor in the School of Engineering, Science, and Technology at Connecticut State University in New Britain, Conn., where he teaches a course on leadership, a unique course that analyzes failures in management decision-making, as well as other courses.

Bob earned a Bachelor of Science degree in mechanical engineering from the University of Miami, a Master's degree in chemical engineering from the University of Rhode Island, and a Ph.D. degree in Engineering from Brown University.

He worked in the consumer products and aerospace industries for 15 years, beginning as a materials engineer. He has held management positions in engineering, manufacturing, and supply chain management at Pratt & Whitney.

Bob joined academia in September 1999 at Rensselaer Polytechnic Institute (Hartford, Connecticut campus) and worked there until 2004. He joined Connecticut State University in 2005. While in academia, he developed the Lean teaching pedagogy and led activities to continuously improve master's degree programs.

Emiliani has authored or co-authored 16 books, four book chapters, and more than 45 peer-reviewed papers. He has received six awards for writing.

Please visit his personal web sites www.bobemiliani.com and www.leanprofessor.com

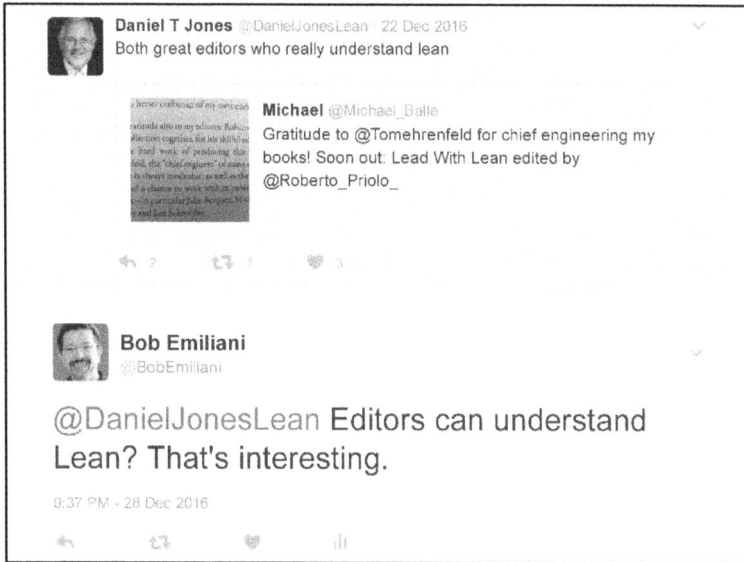

Daniel T Jones @DanielJonesLean · 22 Dec 2016
Both great editors who really understand lean

Michael @Michael_Balle
Gratitude to @Tomehrenfeld for chief engineering my
books! Soon out: Lead With Lean edited by
@Roberto_Priolo_

Bob Emiliani
@BobEmiliani

@DanielJonesLean Editors can understand
Lean? That's interesting.

9:37 PM · 28 Dec 2016

Former Toyota president and chairman Fujio Cho:

"Our way of thinking is very difficult
to copy or even to understand."

Day, P. (2007), "'Mr Toyota' is shy about being No 1," BBC News,
http://news.bbc.co.uk/2/hi/business/6237110.stm, 25 June

Former Toyota president Katsuaki Watanabe:

"There's no end to the process of learning about the Toyota
Way.
I don't think I have a complete understanding even today,
and I have worked for the company for 43 years."

Stewart, T. and Raman, A. (2007), "Lessons from Toyota's Long Drive,"
Harvard Business Review, July-August, p. 80

"Improvement is eternal and infinite."

- Taiichi Ohno

www.ingramcontent.com/pod-product-compliance
Lightning Source LLC
Chambersburg PA
CBHW031932190326
41519CB00007B/496

9780989863179